"Upon opening these pages, the first thing you will find is that this is not a "How To" book but rather it provides many answers to the question "Why?".

Aloia Sensei is a master of the physical art of Aikido and proves in this book to be a master of the written word as well. In here the practitioner will find many truths. Some are not explicit and will become obvious to you only as you progress in your physical understanding of the art. This is a book you will want to read many times on your own journey to mastery. Each reading will reveal something different and at times more profound."

Jerry D. Poole,
Chief Operating Officer, MedRisk, Inc.
Student of Aikido

How Aikido Can Change the World

by Michael Aloia

Aloia Publishing USA
First Edition 2009

How Aikido Can Change the World
Copyright©2009 by Michael Aloia
Aloia Publishing
Collegeville, PA

Disclaimer
The material presented within this book is based on the author's observations and
personal experiences. It is designed as a means to convey a personal opinion. Neither the
publisher nor the author makes any claims, representations, warranty or guarantee to the
success and or the effectiveness of the content described and/or illustrated in this book.

Additional copies are available at *www.asahidojo.com*
Library of Congress Control Number: 2009905519
ISBN 978-0-578-02614-5

Editor: Pamela Aloia
Illustrations: Michael Aloia
Cover Photograph: Jerry Poole & Dillon Poole
Layout Design: Linh Nguyen

Cover Photo Rendering & Design: A Creation Productions *www.acreations.com*

For more information:
Asahikan Dojo
Michael Aloia
Po Box 26452
Collegeville, PA 19426
www.asahidojo.com

Printed in the USA

Dedications

To

my Father –
for always being there in spirit.

Pamela, Antonio and Annelise –
for your constant love and support, always.

Thank You

To

Utada Kancho –
for our time together, your support and your guidance - OSU!

Asahikan Dojo -
for your infinite channels of inspiration

Wa Harmony

How Aikido Can Change the World

Contents

My intention and ambition for writing this book is to relay my experiences and observations given to me from the art of Aikido and how these aspects created for me a new understanding of life and my fellow man.

I am by no means the perfect picture of enlightenment. I stumble just the same as many. Yet it has been through the teachings and the training of Aikido that I have been able to continue forward in my pursuit of enlightenment and life balance.

Aikido is a form of budo – a martial way. For it to truly be effective on all levels, we must practice it as an art - an art that cultivates mind, body and spirit. At times what does not seem effective in the physical sense is actually strengthening what lies inside of us all. Our training is constant balancing of the material world and the spiritual realm. And in between the two is enlightenment. Enlightenment does not need to be some mystical thing or place; it does not need to be an all-knowing sort of thing either. To me, true enlightenment is being at peace with yourself, at peace with others and at peace with the world we live in. So each of us will discover our own form of enlightenment. For some Aikido is that path to enlightenment. For others, it may be ikebana, flower arrangement, or simple gardening. Whatever the road, your fullest attention on you is required.

There is the letter of the art of Aikido and the spirit of the art. The letter tells us there is this way or that way to do things. But the true essence is the spirit of the art. The spirit enables us to be who we are at that moment. Our spirit encourages us to take our current understandings and beliefs and research and challenge them without fear of persecution. It allows us to be.

If we make Aikido our own and allow ourselves to experience new heights of freedom in thinking and doing, we will create a world of beauty and harmony. You will not be disappointed.

With this undertaking, I have drawn from countless hours of training, the teachings of my sensei - past and present, from my sempai, from my peers, from my students and from reflection within.

To all of whom were with me along the way – thank you. Osu!

- Michael Aloia

introduction

When confronted with adversity – be it physical, mental, emotional or spiritual confrontation – there are two common human reactions. The first type of reaction is to turn and run away. Here, fear takes hold of us and we try to avoid what we are in conflict with. In this case, we never face or address the cause of the fear, and in turn, never face the conflict.

The second type of reaction is to meet the confrontation head on – to fiercely oppose what is given to us – fighting back with our own arsenal of beliefs, opinions and experiences. Such a response results in a war of attrition, where the duelers extract an 'eye-for-an-eye', and we end up with a situation where no one is truly victorious.

Naturally, both reactions end with no peaceful resolution in sight.

There is a third path, one that is least commonly used. The third path uses a mechanism whereby one can gain a deeper understanding of the opponent - a system of values and principles designed to create harmony and peace and further the relationship. It is called Aikido, a Japanese martial art created by O Sensei, Morihei Ueshiba, during the 1940s.

Aikido is the Way of Harmony. It is an opportunity to view a situation from a multitude of perspectives; to hone in on the mindset of your adversary, as well as yourself; a chance to effectively reconcile the differences the world clings to. The Aikido approach resolves tensions that lead to divisions and diminishes the hostile feelings that are simmering at the root of all conflict.

Aikido's basic philosophy can be summed up as taking the time to see the other person's side. Much like the old saying "if you walked a mile in my shoes..." If we took the time to see life through the eyes of the person we deem to be the enemy or the opposition, we may come to a new understanding as to why the situation has arisen, or why someone acts the way they do, or better yet why we act the way we do.

The principles of Aikido apply equally well to the conflicts we encounter within ourselves. Although Aikido can be regarded as a way to reconcile the difference with others, Aikido is also a way to reconcile from within. The art fosters introspection, making us mull our purpose – to carefully consider our role – to others, to the world and to ourselves.

Aikido focuses not so much on the differences we may have, but more on the similarities and on how these similarities can conjoin, creating a much stronger, well-balanced series of movements. And through these movements, each individual involved in a conflict, learns and experiences life through the eyes of another. The subtleties in life are embraced and built upon, enriching every ounce of who we are and what we will become. It takes our thinking into new directions and on new plains, reaching new plateaus – opening our eyes, ears and hearts to the wonder of existence and the relationship we have with all that exists.

Aikido is more than a journey – it is a way of doing, a way of being, a way of feeling and a way of relating. We learn to relate to what matters most – our personal faith and beliefs, our family, our friends and our dreams. We learn to take pleasure in the small things, basking in the subtleties of life. We do away with all needless things such as greed and envy. We encompass the best of what life itself has to offer; we are giving back our best everyday. We become children again; as each day unfolds, we learn and experience new information. Our experiences create a chain reaction. This domino effect is felt by everyone we encounter and all that we touch. One experience causes yet another new experience allowing this powerful cycle to continue. We must be open to the endless possibilities of what one idea can do for the present and even more for the future.

The essential Aikido principle is simple: if something is coming at you – move or embrace it. If you want, you can become one with the opposing force; if you do not want to do this, you also have the option of redirecting the opposing force and letting it pass you by harmlessly. Within that moment of embracement, we have the opportunity to view in meticulous detail what it is that we are being confronted with. Being able to view a situation from another perspective affords great insight and a better understanding of another and of ourselves. For just that moment we are the other person – the very thing itself that we have been confronted with – we are given a precious gift - a chance to connect with another. This instant sharing of space, time and thought creates a bond of trust by allowing another into your world; a moment to see life through each other's eyes – to walk that mile. And in that instant something incredible happens – our understanding of the world increases and clarity takes hold. Through a simple gesture of connection we are enlightened. And we have been enlightened – just by taking the time to connect.

Our memories are based on experiences, experiences that involve the world around us. Why not positively touch what is around us so to create an endless series of positive experiences and lasting memories?

The Aikido philosophy applies to both our words and actions, so it is important that we always speak positively. Life is a series of experiences –many of which are verbal, not physical. Staying positive is being open to all the facts. And to be open to all the facts we must look at a situation from the other side. At times it is always hard to see the big picture but the more information we have, the less likely we will be to over-react and make judgments.

Aikido in its purest form teaches this concept through movement. Through the use of tenkan – a circle stepping – we approach confrontation or conflict by first stepping towards it and then moving around to the side or behind it. We end up with the vantage point of the aggressor. We now see what they see. To overcome a challenge we must face the challenge. To face it we must embrace it. And to embrace it we must become one with it. Only then are we truly capable of understanding it and only then will we know how to deal with it - we must become *one* with it.

In Aikido, much depends on the mental outlook and frame of mind as one acts. As you develop a focused and well-balanced physical structure and form, you are also developing a fine-tuned and calm way of thinking. Your mind takes on new levels of interpreting situations and reactions. We learn to read our environment before any physical action has taken place.

The mere fact that we have mentally chosen to attend a class and forego our comfort zone shows a strong level of commitment. The body then becomes an instrument, a means for carrying out what the mind and heart wish to accomplish.

This mental supremacy can and will carry over into other facets of everyday life. We learn to view our surroundings, our environment, in a new way, not to look for trouble but to become aware of its presence and also the possibilities to avoid it.

This mind awareness training lends its help in daily routines. For instance - how we interact with one another, or assessing a situation before we choose to become involved it - that is mental readiness. Rather than simply avoiding an irate customer or an aggravated spouse, we move towards them and get closer to them. While it may be easier to avoid them altogether, the Aikido way recognizes that interaction is necessary with our surroundings regardless of the state of affairs. So what are we to do when confronted with an unpleasant person or situation? With mental readiness we avoid the rough spots and center in on the positive – control the situation by blending to subdue. Do not look to feed the negative to an issue, but enter in and look at things from that person's perspective. Why are they doing this? Why are they reacting this way? What can I offer? Learn the facts.

Knowledge is powerful. The more we know, the more we grow.

Tolerance has more to do with knowing the facts rather than just accepting people and things at face value. Knowledge is powerful. The more we know, the more we grow. When we interact on the training mat, we have come under the umbrella of learning; to learn what we can from the Sensei – the instructor – and also from each student and from ourselves. We go to push our limits to better understanding. Why not do the same in everyday life? In a class, a student is taught to do the following – when one is pushed, pull. And when one is pulled, push. We must do this in life as well. Aikido does not teach to push back when pushed or pull when pulled – that is a primitive response based in fear, a kind where there is no blending - no chance to see or feel what the other person does.

Rather than meet someone head-to-head with opposition, use the opportunity to learn and grow. Learn to know another. To know them is to be them in a way that creates harmony for all. We reach new levels in the relationship, if we ourselves and those we connect with, give a reason to interact positively - a purpose to connect and become one. Together we learn, together we grow.

Society has made a living at exposing the general conflict of mankind. Be it man versus nature, man versus the unknown or man versus man, struggle has become a huge source of revenue. Fueled by a world that craves more, we are always looking for the differences to make us stand apart. In Aikido the way to subdue or control a violent attack is to find the similarities. And in this case it is the movement that takes place. The aggressor, called uke in Aikido, creates an attack through some form of movement. On the other side is the nage, the thrower or defender. Nage sees this movement and responds in the same manner – with movement. But movement alone might not subdue or control the attack. It does, however, create time – a chance for a second encounter – a second impression, without causing harm to anyone involved. But to begin to subdue or control the attack made by uke, nage must first blend with the movement and become one with the movement, not the person or the intent, but with the movement that has been created. Once nage has blended, the two motions become one and nage needs to decide to direct or redirect the now amplified movement. The movement is amplified since nage and uke's movements are now one – the circle of power intensifies. If nage directs the attack, leading it in its original direction, nage creates an opportunity for a second encounter. It also gives way for nage to make a quick escape in the opposite direction. But if nage connects and chooses to redirect the attack, this redirection diffuses the attack rendering it powerless, so now nage has created a new situation, under a new set of rules. Under these rules, called nage's lead, falls degrees of control, whereby nage must decide, based on the severity of the attack, intent or situation, how far to take the execution of technique. Do they send a subtle message "please do not try this again"? Or, do they go to extremes where injury or possible death could occur? Aikido helps us make these types of choices, putting situations in proper perspective to properly respond.

With power comes responsibility, and just because you can does not mean you should. Aikido teaches that to obtain a better world we must learn to harmonize with who or what resides in it. We are all creatures of God and should be treated as such – regardless of what your idea of God is, this principle of harmonization can take place in everyday life – in everyday encounters – no matter how big or small.

When confronted with a hostile individual or situation, we have the ability to lead it, redirect it and make it better. No one gets hurt. Mutual respect is maintained and everyone learns. We learn something about ourselves. We learn we can make things better – one situation at a time, one encounter at a time, one person at a time. Why not practice this daily? Make it part of what we do – make it who we are. If everyone took the time, the world would be a better place. One person can make a difference.

Day in Day Out
Aikido is more than a study of motion or a science of self-defense; it has evolved into a means of human interaction. How we deal with it, how we perceive it, how we relate to it and how we respond to it. Human interaction is a multi faceted collection of past, present and future involvements. It is a game of pool that is played on an emotional level and the stakes are acceptance. But before we can seek acceptance from others we must first come to accept ourselves - for who and what we are. To understand others, we must understand ourselves – both our strengths and limitations.

Aikido, though rooted in ancient ideology, is a marvel in modern martial arts. The art has become so innovative and diversified, it is not practiced the same anywhere. Aikido has lent itself to become as individual as the individual who practices it. The art has found its way into every possible form, relying more on opportunity and function and less on style and technique. The principles of Aikido are not unique, but they are special. Others preach their value and validity but few actually follow through in applying them to routine training let alone daily life.

Aikido has proven its adaptability as worldwide interest has peaked. Aikido functions as a base source, a benchmark, for art excellence. As martial artists have found their way to Aikido, Aikido has found its way into other arts. The mere idea of including the thoughts and approaches of Aikido's philosophy and technique seems to give other arts and styles a deeper meaning, a deeper purpose, a sense of history or legacy. As it increases the awareness of Aikido, it also creates a vision of what Aikido is not, sometimes misleading the public. This happens when individuals just graze the surface, taking only face value of what they see. These primitive or premature interpretations are then incorporated with other surface findings and strung together into executing techniques, possibly creating a new "art". Again this can become misleading to viewers and new students. When asked what this is, the response, "this is Aikido." What Aikido is and can be goes far beyond the simple execution of "Aikido style" techniques. It truly is a way of thinking, feeling and being. Not winning, losing or being able to destroy another or thing.

So simply "just doing" may not be enough to capture the true essence. Consider the intent. How will this affect both my partner and me? Is this for the greater good of all involved? What have I learned about them, about myself? Applying and executing technique correctly is just the first level of understanding the effects of Aikido in your life – the physical level. The more you do it the more you change. The more you learn and the less you understand. Aggressive tendencies seem to taper off. Where there was once anger and frustration, patience now exists. A belief that the impossible is possible strengthens our faith and convictions – it makes us believe. Aikido makes us stronger – in every way. A simple decision to begin the path leads to a journey of never ending discoveries and new possibilities – inner and outer- level upon level. How is this achieved? Where does this magic lie? What do I need to do?

The answer is two fold. First through consistent training in the art, many questions are answered. Repetition has a miraculous way of filling in the blanks. To keep those blanks filled in, we must continue to repeat. As with anything, repetition builds character, strength, clarity, focus, confidence and power. It also challenges us by asking "what if?" And again through constant training, those "what if" questions are also answered, providing us with discipline, reasoning, a stronger faith, a deeper sense of purpose and knowledge. All of which are rewards that we pass to others through our experience and interaction. The art also helps us confront our fears and misconceptions – many relating to gender, race, religion, size, muscle strength, pride, ego, humility, worthiness and coordination. The art challenges us to face those fears and misconceptions head on starting with ourselves. Much of what we find is shallow and uneducated reasons and beliefs. In many cases to make things work we must do nothing at all - so we learn to just be.

> *To begin* you must *have courage.*
>
> *To learn* you must *have patience.*
>
> *To succeed* you must *have discipline.*
>
> *To progress* you must *be humble.*

Since we are all beginners, we quickly learn humility. Humility leads to an understanding of sacrifice. Through sacrifice we become balanced. When training with another, we are repeatedly giving ourselves for the purpose of learning – thus, sacrificing. We let go of our bodies, minds, ego and time. In turn our partners do the same. This is the journey – the journey of self-discovery through interaction – an interaction that leads to learning and growing.

So to simply repeat a movement or technique and call is Aikido is missing the mark. There is more.

The flip side is that Aikido is everything – all arts, all styles, all beliefs. What makes Aikido unique, again, is intent. This intent provides the foundations as to how and why, not merely who and what.

The Proof

If the proof of the pudding is in the taste, than the proof of Aikido is in the execution. However, before that proof can take place, training needs to occur – proper training. Training is the cause to create the effect. It is the means to an end – though the true end can never be reached. By this we mean there is always another level, something more to learn – to learn of ourselves – true learning is endless. With our training we are in a constant state of growth and discovery. And only through training is development achieved. What we need to learn can only be found through our training. Through exhausted diligence do answers present themselves to us. We work towards perfection. We strive to be flawless. If we think we are perfect or flawless then our training has stopped – we no longer grow. We have closed our minds and our hearts to the possibilities that lie ahead. We have allowed our ego to take control rather than us controlling it. Ironically, the perception of being perfect is a flaw itself. Even those who have been "enlightened" continue to strive to higher realms. It is the search that fuels the drive. The discoveries fuel the tireless search.

Many practitioners begin training at the end. Whereby they see the Founder in his final years – effortless, relaxed, almost magical in his applications. Without thought, students dive into a training routine to copy this without realizing the time it took to achieve such a level - the countless trial and error, experimentation and sacrifice to learn. It is a collection of time and experience that shines through. Through these experiences one is able to achieve and display such levels. To forego them is depriving us of our own experiences.

Many of us want to be considered advanced. We are impatient. Our ego says we do not need to begin at the beginning. But at the beginning is where we are introduced to what lies ahead. A necessary step to achieving that "advanced level".

We instruct new students to approach learning as a large funnel, where the mouth is at the top. As we begin and continue on our journey we must take all the information we can: good, bad, right, wrong, hard, soft, fast, slow, from whomever and where ever. As we progress, the funnel opening gets smaller – this is where we begin to process our collected information. We use what resonates with us – both inward and outward. Until we reach the point that it needs to come out – the end of the funnel. We find that to be "advanced" we must be basic and basic is where the beginner's mind prevails. All great masters possess a strong sense of the *basics. But as learning dictates to truly understand the basics we must learn* a variety of applications and scenarios to foster the ability to own them within our movements. In Aikido it is often seen among the long time practitioners that kokyunage, timing or breath throw, is executed most often. It is the timing of the movement and the simplicity of the motion that affords the fastest route. It is the least amount of force or energy needed to deliver the strongest effect – the most bang for the buck idea.

The funnel approach creates a *waste not, want not* cycle. It's all in there, use only what you need, when you need it. No more, no less. Aikido, in its theory of effective, efficient movement is the same – don't use more than what you need to do the technique but no less as not to make it work and result in the use of strength. Judo coined the phrase "maximum efficiency, minimal effort."

The above phrase pertains to execution of technique not necessarily to training. If we train with minimal efforts, we allow our bodies to control who we are. Some will say we become soft. Our bodies will always take the easy way out. If allowed, our bodies will overpower our minds, thus, losing all control. We will have become puppets or slaves to depression, laziness and pain. To make maximum efficiency with minimal efforts, our minds and bodies must be in balance. Balance can be achieved through training. One feeds off the other - when things are perceived as good and when things are perceived as bad. We work towards the balance – everyday, every hour, every minute. It is our strength and it is our weakness. Balance is what we seek but what few ever find.

Balancing Act

When we seek balance we seek stability - stability in our lives, stability within ourselves, and stability with others. Stability in Aikido begins with our stance. Everything begins and ends in kamae – our stance. Without a solid stance, a strong foundation, everything else will crumble. Movement would be futile if we are not stable. Stability begins with trust – trust in ourselves, in our decisions, trust in who we are and trust in what we can become. Stability relies on letting go and just being. Here many of us falter because we put up barriers blocking who we are thus blocking who and what we can become. If we cannot trust ourselves, we will never be able to trust others. Trust in Aikido is the backbone of learning and progression. Without trust in our partners we will never achieve the flow and connection needed to become successful. Of course that trust needs to be gained on both ends. As you can see it all ties together – one is nothing without the other. Balance is stability, stability is trust and trust is growth - all essential parts of the collective whole.

Together, they are but one aspect and nothing more than a fraction of a greater good - one that without each component would be nonfunctional. Hence, each part should be balanced in relationship to itself as well as being balanced to the whole - mental, physical, emotional and spiritual stability, trusting yourself and others. Balance the mind and the body, inner and outer – growing internally as well as externally. As in Aikido, we should be open to receive.

By placing ourselves in another's shoes, we challenge our own understandings, views and beliefs by accepting those of someone else. In Aikido the constant changing of roles creates a balance of thought. As we change partners, we are given a new view to accept - and as technique is changed, yet another view; different instructor, still another new set of views and so on. Constantly building our character and eliminating any predisposed judgments we may have. Thus, we are truly receiving. To receive we must accept it as a gift. If it is not accepted as a gift, then one just takes. Taking is a forced action, either from another or upon one's self. Whereas accepting is a mutual gratification – it is wanted or needed. Everyone wants to be wanted or needs to be needed - a basic human desire - though many of us choose to alienate ourselves as well as those around us. We take an important human component out of our existence, which leads to an unbalanced state. To be successful as uke or nage in Aikido, we must learn to receive the energy given to us by our partners. We must want to blend and create the need to do so - in each role, blending with the energy – accepting it. The energies balance themselves out through this acceptance. This connection of the energies plays a pivotal role in the channeling of both internal and external power. Without it we have nothing but a series of movements. As we take turns, accepting each role, we come closer to enhancing our constant state of balance. This balance carries over in all we do. When we are offered something in life - in Aikido, another's trust - we need to decide if we wish to accept this offering. If so, we receive it with an open mind and open heart. If we would rather not or if it is being forced upon us to take, our next option would be to let it pass by getting out of the way. Within Aikido the simple act of getting out of the way and moving on is called yoke (yo – kay) – evading. We can choose to move and see it from another perspective until we feel the need to apply technique or we just get out of the way and move on.

All of this happens within an instant. In our beginning stages we walk through it step by step. We are given directions and cues on how to move and respond. We are guided through at a pace that is understandable and obtainable. It is through these humbling beginnings that we are introduced to responding by feeling. Being able to feel tends to lead to faster response times. Feeling the move will inevitably surpass seeing the move. Our early learning creates an awareness to signals that leads to being able to feel. We are taught what to look for and how to respond. Once we are aware, we look past seeing and work towards feeling. Feel the change in uke's position, feel the direction of nage's lead, feel when to advance or move back, feel when center is broken. We learn to feel the intent. This focus takes us deeper into the depths of human existence and understanding. We can learn what makes others tick. We begin to relate past the physical and more towards the internal levels. Once the spirit and the mind are focused and in tune, they are unstoppable. It is a force to be reckoned with, one that makes the impossible possible.

How we choose to deal with a situation will determine the outcome. If we are flexible yet focused and confident, we will succeed, whereas a hesitant, doubtful and cowering approach leads to the opposite – in Aikido and in life.

Releasing ourselves from past demons and hang-ups will ensure a balanced state. We must let go to be able to move forward - let go to go. Energy is just that – energy. We make it good or bad by our intent, focus and judgment. If we focus on things that have brought us sadness and hurt, then the energy will have negative effects on us and what lies before us. But by letting go and understanding that past times of trials and tribulations are but a fraction of what we have done and not who we are and what we can become, we can forgive ourselves and others and move on. Good or bad moments of our lives have shaped who we are right now and who we are is always the best we can be ever. Let go and move on.

As Aikido digs deeper into our very essence of existence, we find that positive provoking thought is in all we do. Negative thoughts and actions are quickly snuffed out. A better you, a better me philosophy prevails.

Aikido, at its core, is learning a new perspective and taking that new perspective and applying it to our lives. We realize with our newly found views we have a source to draw strength from. We learn to physically move from our center but all the while everything we do and say, how we act and react, moves from the center within, and we become stabilized. This stabilization provides the footing to withstand anything that comes our way. Aikido stresses good rooted stances – rooted but mobile. If we are not mobile, then we are not prepared for change – change of flow, change of direction and change of mind. We must be connected to the earth through our stance. This connection creates a strong stance but also aids in generating power when we are required to move. Like a swimmer pushing off the side of a pool during a race, it propels them in the direction they want to go. This connection to the earth does the same for the Aikido-ka during movement.

We must always be moving forward, even if we are required to step back, our intention, our focus and center is still moving forward. Sometimes to continue ahead we must take a step back. We have not changed the destination or the intent but rather have modified the journey. This happens often in Aikido training. Even within technique, we can allow things to pass if we choose. Our choice creates options and options open doors.

Aikido becomes a new way of finding yourself - a new way of interacting with others and our surroundings. Aikido is a life changing, full body experience that opens our hearts and minds to the wonders of the world.

I. What is Aikido?

Aikido is as individual as the individual who takes on the journey. On the surface Aikido is a Japanese martial art designed to defend one's self against oncoming aggression - achieved by moving out of the way of an attack and absorbing that energy as part of our own - becoming one to diffuse the situation. This takes years of diligent and self-disciplined training under the proper guidance. At the same time we condition our bodies to be well-oiled machines ready to take on any physical challenge set before us. There is no training like Aikido training some may say. Over time as we meet one physical challenge after another, we find our technique grows stronger. We come to understand the use of proper center. Center being the area of a person's being that possess great strength and balance. We learn to control our bodies and move with minimal effort while producing the maximum effects. Our mind and body become one and our spirit is unbreakable.

But, Aikido is not a parlor trick filled with only physical feats. For many practitioners it takes on a deeper meaning. Aikido becomes a new way of finding yourself - a new way of interacting with others and our surroundings. Aikido is a life changing, full body experience that opens our hearts and minds to the wonders of the world. This aspect of Aikido training is much more difficult to achieve. Aikido is a life long journey that challenges us every minute of everyday. We must take the teachings we learn in the dojo, a setting designed for formal physical, mental and spiritual training, and apply them to everyday life and beyond the physical sense.

As a beginner student of Aikido, we are not aware of the hidden positive effects Aikido has on us. We are consumed with learning what the sensei demonstrated and work hard to imitate what we have seen, practicing it over and over again – pushing the physical boundaries. All the while, though, we are learning conflict resolution techniques that can change our perspectives and behavior on human relations. As we train in Aikido we experience the role as both the attacker and defender. This allows us to learn how to react from both sides – learning to see what another sees - through role reversal training. When we take the time to find out where others are coming from we learn something of ourselves. We learn to be patient, tolerant, understanding and compassionate. We focus on the similarities and not the differences. And by focusing on the similarities we learn to expound on the benefits and what they have to offer and the changes they can make. Far too often what is really important gets lost in an effort to be dominant or in control – only by what we say or do. Aikido teaches us to give way because all has something to offer even though it may be different. Through understanding what is different we can find what is the same in us all.

Aikido is more than a way to defend one's self. Aikido is more than a Japanese art form. Aikido is a way of being - a way of living - a way to express one's self and a way of thinking. Aikido takes on a personal meaning unique to all involved. Aikido becomes an expression of life, a journey leading to better understanding through open communication, which allows us to think and react with others in a positive and nurturing light. We find that we learn from one another, we grow together, bridging the conflict of differences through a mutual acceptance of each other and what we have to offer.

Aikido training is a series of peaks and valleys. Peaks being the energetic, all encompassing high points whereas the valleys are the times when we feel confused, frustrated and lost, as if we have learned nothing. For many of us we may seem to spend an awful amount of time in the valleys. Life by its natural design also follows this series of peaks and valleys. Some things are unavoidable - sickness, disease and death. Many things are avoidable. We need to decide a proper course of living that keeps us more on the peaks and less in the valleys. What we choose and how we choose can be a major influence. Within Aikido training what we choose and how we choose to deal with an attack impacts the outcome. As we mentioned before, if an attack is coming in faster than we like or unexpectedly, rather than muddle through a lack luster response, we can simply choose to avoid it and take it from another direction or view point – one that puts us in proper position. We then can choose again to intercept it with technique, take yet another view point or walk away. Life holds these same options for us – we just need to make the choice. Not everything needs to be met head on or at first encounter. At times quick and rash actions can put us in a far worse position or state of mind. We must deal with situations one step at a time - focusing on the moment. If we venture only in the outcome, we have missed the moments in between – what has lead us to this point. More often than we realize most negative confrontation can be avoided. If we employ the principles of time and space, giving ourselves ample time to assess the issue, while creating the space to maintain proper, safe distance, we increase the positive. In Aikido one affords the other and is referred to as "ma ai" – mutual distance. Space creates time and time makes space. "Haste", as the saying goes, "makes waste", stripping us of both precious time and needed space.

Go With the Flow

Aikido is about many things: defending against an oncoming attack, our interaction with one another, dealing with our daily routines, dealing with ourselves or challenging ourselves and others to be better people. All of us have our reasons for training in Aikido and no doubt all different. Whatever the reason, our training brings us together for a short time everyday. Bonds are made, trust is developed and an understanding of how another thinks, acts and feels is gained. These bonds of trust help attribute to a greater state of life, a better and more positive attitude that will surely affect others - not only on how they treat us but also how they treat others and themselves. A positive mind spawns a positive environment. And in a positive environment, growth occurs. This is what training in Aikido, on or off the mat, is all about. Positive energy makes positive people making a positive environment. This strengthens our bonds, enhances the trust and clarifies our understanding - all for the greater good. So remember the next time you are on the mat or about your daily routine, it's not about who is bigger, stronger, wealthier, faster, or more athletic, it's not about age, sex or religious beliefs, it's about going with the flow of what is happening right then and there with the others around you. How will you build on that?

II. Connection
- Becoming One

Connection is at the heart of the Aikido ideology. Without this key element, the mere practice of physical technique would be futile. Thus, Aikido as it was designed would be ineffective. When we connect we join energies with whom or what we embrace. Through this connection we are able to become one, including becoming one with ourselves.

To fully understand connection, we must realize that connection has many levels. The first levels are a state of mind and a state of being. Though normally what is visually seen in training is a connection of the physical states – a form of states of being – being in physical contact. Connection does not have to be just physical. Take for instance a monk who spends a good portion of his time in silent meditation. This meditation transcends the physical. This kind of connection supercedes the physical to the spiritual and sometimes beyond. It is the connection with other levels of consciousness and understanding that has been developed. This connection requires us to let go and experience. Aikido offers us this opportunity.

Awareness of Connection
Awareness, then, has to do more with understanding your surroundings than simply seeing what is around you. Yes, it is important to visually recognize potentially dangerous situations or individuals but sometimes that may not give you enough time to react properly. By broadening our senses we can become in tune with our surroundings on a higher vibrational level – a level that can forewarn us of a circumstance we would want to avoid, perhaps a sixth sense, if you will. All things living or not give off vibrations/emotions – energy. If we learn to connect with these vibrations we can become more aware of what is around us.

Utilize the connection Aikido teaches to become aware of negative aggression. Connect with it, but do not become it. Negative aggression can consume you if you allow it. Awareness allows for options.

Levels of Connection
With Aikido practice, we should then look to make connection before we physically touch our partner. Connect vibrationally then

visually – feelings, intent, environment, size, shape, etc., of our partner, the situation and the surroundings.

We then make a mental connection. And with this mental connection we determine how the technique will unfold. We can either make or break the technique simply by our mindset. All the physical connection from that point on will not help us if we have

Understand what is taking place and what may take place. This understanding is a means of creating balance within.

not made this mental level connection. We must make the mental commitment to follow through with what we started. We accept our role and the role of our partner. On the mat we share the role of teacher and student – helping to learn and grow. In a violent situation our role could be a matter of life or death. Our mental connection to the two extremes or what lies in between is our key to success. Understand what is taking place and what may take place. This understanding is a means of creating balance within. And this balance carries over without - it is stability, it is our foundation.

From here it is a matter of movement – physical connection - whereas nage executes technique, all the while maintaining our previous levels of connection.

The initial mindset, or intent, is what creates the state of being in all that we do and in all that we set out to accomplish.

Staying Connected
During every Aikido technique we practice, uke and nage must stay connected with the movement and each other.

Uke can achieve this by:
- committing to their attack
- flowing with the defensive technique executed by nage
- executing their own defense with ukemi

Nage must follow similar rules.
- connect and blend with uke's attack
- keep a continuous lead with the technique – do not stop moving
- follow through completing the circle or to some form of pin
  when applicable.

Staying connected is a cornerstone in achieving the essence of Aikido. Staying connected ensures uke does not escape or counter and aides to the converging of energies from nage and uke, thus, increasing the power of technique. For uke, staying connected helps to execute good ukemi, creates awareness and provides direction. For nage, staying connected offers the ability to sense and feel the surroundings, helps to stay focused and stills the mind.

Connection also gives Aikido-ka a point of reference, which allows for stability and centering of ki. Connection can be described as a form of Zen. It is a plateau that Aikido-ka of all ranks strive to acquire yet few achieve consistently. It is this search for connection that keeps the journey of learning fueled with the desire to continue. Staying connected is a philosophy that can be used on and off the mat.

As we mentioned before connection is a form of balance. To be balanced everything must be aligned and if we are aligned we are connected. It is a continuous circle.

Connection gives us a heightened sense of subtle changes in the things going on around us – family, friends, circumstances that arise. These subtle changes can go unnoticed if we are not tuned in – not connected. But when we are connected we are able to respond, adapt, modify and blend.

Blending is something that cannot be taught. It can be shown and sometimes explained but it has to be felt.

III. Blending
- Moving with

Since Aikido has to do with connection, we as practitioners must learn to blend with one another. We must work together to achieve the same goal. Some progress at different rates, processing information as it is understood or needed. To truly achieve the higher levels we must learn how to yield to the needs of others. We must learn to give of ourselves for the betterment of others - both on and off the mat. In turn we learn something not just of technique but also of ourselves.

Aikido teaches us cooperation. We learn this by working with one another as nage and uke.

In the beginning stages of learning the "why" part may be a bit over our heads. But we learn the deeper meaning of techniques only after we fully understand "what" we are doing and have practiced it over and over again. We train with many different uke - different body types, different intents and different understandings. Different uke allow us to experience the different effects of the same technique - opening ourselves to the hidden qualities of technique and a stronger grasp of understanding – allowing us to find our own way and discovering the "why".

This process is often frustrating, but allow time and experience to be your guide. Blending is something that cannot be taught. It can be shown and sometimes explained but it has to be felt. It is a "do". Constant training and awareness is the only way to get there.

In Aikido it is the basics that get us to where we want to be. As we progress through ranks we may get fancier and flashier with technical approaches and executions. There comes a time when we revert to what really matters - the basics of movement. All the great masters implement proper use of the basics - simplifying the movement, becoming faster and stronger. So to grow we must accept what is simple. Once we know that, we are free to let go and just be. We have then blended with ourselves on a higher level.

Each new level starts us on a new path of learning and discovery - new challenges - new ideas. We learn something not only of technique but of ourselves as well. Always keep an open mind and a pure, humble heart.

It is when we reach the end that we must begin again.

Blend to Modify

What if Aikido techniques do not work? To what degree of alteration do we need to include if uke does not follow through with their role? This all depends on the connection nage made with uke. Nage must again be able to blend with the situation. If one technique does not work, go into another or if they are stopped in one direction, move into another direction. If movement has stopped, create it again. Aikido is based on the premise of capturing and recapturing another's energy - blending with it and redirecting it. This is true for many of the kokyunage (breath throw) techniques. Find the path of least resistance through blending.

The principles of Aikido can be applied to all aspects of life without fail. However, at times they may need to be modified, tweaked and regularly practiced. First they need to be learned - learned how to do them and learned how to feel them. All great athletes just do - they feel what to do at that given moment - it is reaction not action – it is part of them. Reaction is much faster than action. Action is a thought, reaction is response. Through regular training our reaction becomes a tailored response becoming part of our overall make up.

For us to truly learn both as uke and nage, we must give it our all so both learn, both grow. Nage needs to be aware of uke's intent - meaning they should only respond with as much energy that has been given by uke. Nage must be able to sense the amount of energy and go with it - not to throttle through to the finish, especially if the attack does not warrant it. This sensitivity to respond takes time to develop and will develop as long as nage stays aware, relaxed and blends.

As for uke, this is where we must hone our defensive skills of falling – our ukemi. Many people forget that ukemi is the other, if not the most important, part of our art - learning to defend ourselves in the event that we are countered, attacked or knocked off balance. Uke needs to sense nage's movement, feel the lead and blend with the motion. Not waiting until there is no other choice but to fall.

There is a small instance during technique where the uke and nage roles are reversed. Just getting out of the way from an oncoming attack is a form of ukemi. We have blended with the attack and given ourselves a way out. So until we make the physical connection to execute our technique we are uke. From there we then become nage - this of course, in a traditional sense is open for discussion but puts things in somewhat of a different perspective opening new channels of learning and discovery.

But since Aikido is considered a "defensive art" then we are always the role of uke – receiving what the world gives us until we choose to diffuse the situation, thus, becoming nage. To what degree we diffuse the situation depends on our level of training, skill and intent and can only come with practice. We need to train the spectrum to grow. Work with fully committed uke, hesitant or resistant uke, beginner and advanced. It all teaches us how, why, when and to what degree to blend and respond.

Blend to Improvise
There will be times when we execute a technique and find ourselves lost, our minds go blank. How can we have just forgotten what Sensei demonstrated? Some may fumble through a solution while trying to regain control and in the process give up balance and resort to strength to save technique only to execute it poorly. The opportunity to blend has been missed.

A good training exercise to aid us to remedy this sort of situation is called henka waza (multiple techniques). In this exercise, uke gives a good committed but a slower controlled paced attack and nage's job is to respond in turn with a series of techniques that flow from one to another while attempting to stay focused, balanced and in control. This is a sort of randori (free practice) type of exercise. The only difference is we are working with one uke rather than three or more. This exercise challenges our mind and body to think and work together - to focus – to feel - to respond to the unknown and unexpected - to push our creativity to the maximum – to blend.

When beginning this free style exercise, begin with one attack and execute three good techniques, one flowing into the next, then finish. Allow uke time to react to and absorb your movements and yourself time to do the same. Have uke attack from both sides executing the same three techniques. Once you feel even more comfortable try several opponents, randori style. You will find that if and when those momentary losses of memory occur, you will respond naturally and relaxed because you have blended.

You will find that if and when those momentary losses of memory occur, you will respond naturally and relaxed because you have blended.

IV. Movement
- Relationship with Motion

Movement - our relationship with motion

Martial arts are a constant study in and of motion. Many of us begin not really knowing how to move properly. But through continuous training and repetitive structure, we establish a foundation of movement and motion that becomes natural for us. We develop the means to get out of the way of any oncoming attack or advance.

Movement is the key. Movement allows us our defense, thus movement is our first defense, just not being there. Movement buys us time, though only fractions of a second, enough time to avoid harm's way. Movement creates and closes distance. Movement sets position. Movement creates an escape. Sometimes just moving may be the only defense we need.

We must keep in mind that our number one priority is our protection – regardless of the degree of the threat. This mindset has to be in the forward of our thinking.

So to protect ourselves we must not be where the attack is coming. This is accomplished simply by moving.

When we begin our training, learning to move should set the pace. Everything will stem from the practice of proper movement.

One should always assume that movement takes place naturally. Meaning to get from here to there or there to here we must move. So if you need to reach a target or not be the target – you must move! Aikido teaches us methods of efficient movement.

Let go of using muscle and strength to apply technique. Movement in itself is pure technique.

One can spend a lifetime learning how to move. As we change so does the way we move. So many things factor into how we move; environment, emotions, health, physical and mental states, etc., and together with change, we must constantly train our bodies to move naturally and efficiently.

Aikido involves movement. Movement, no matter how great or small, is the predominant factor in the successful execution of any technique. Simply by moving we evade the initial attack, allow ourselves time and create openings for defense. Movement gives us an edge by not allowing our partner to fix on our position or for counter attack. Aikido is designed to teach us this.

All movement is good though some more efficient than others. In the beginning we move in whatever way necessary. This at least begins us on the path of function. As our training progresses, we must learn to make certain, more economical movements. In time and with continuous training, we find that we do not need to dwell on the thought of movement as much as we did when we began. It becomes instinctual. The movement becomes part of us and we become part of it. Without movement we lose a core principle of Aikido. We will begin to rely on strength. Aikido is movement and movement is Aikido.

As partners, allow each other time to react and absorb the movements. Learn to feel what is happening – sense the movement. Connect with the motion of your partner as well as the technique.

Everything we do is based on the movements we make. Entering, breaking of balance and execution all involve movement. Timing and speed are the result of proper, well-defined movement.

As we become more in tune with our movements the better our techniques will become and the better we will become. By focusing on our movements we understand what we have to offer to Aikido, an art that is in constant motion.

Without Strength
We can easily fall into resorting to the use of strength to apply technique. No doubt, many of us are blessed with incredible amounts of strength. So when it comes to lugging logs or cement bags this strength will come in handy. As far as Aikido training goes it can be an obstacle that hinders learning. Aikido is based on the blending of energy. Connecting with that energy - amplifying it and making it part of our own movement until such time we see fit to release it. Sounds as easy as walking on water, yes, but we must remember that first and foremost when approaching a technique

we must be relaxed - both mind and body. A relaxed state will allow us to move freely and focus on the technique. Once we begin using strength we are no longer relaxed. We have committed our own focus to a single location - our mind, our hands, our arms etc. Once we commit our own focus, how do we then blend with the energy of another? We don't. It then becomes a wrestling match and in most cases the stronger individual will prevail. From this we can learn nothing. We must be in the moment but not get caught up in it. The moment quickly becomes the past. And if we are caught up in, we will miss what is happening now.

As we age our strength will lessen and when used too often, we grow tired. Running out of steam while attempting to defend ourselves is generally not a good thing. Approach technique as if you were without strength. Enter only with motion, allowing the motion to guide you through what you have learned. Let go of using muscle and strength to apply technique. Movement in itself is pure technique.

Strength in Technique
We have all been guilty of rushing through technique to find that we have lost the lead and control, uke has gained back their balance, and to make the technique work we resort to strength. Sometimes it works and other times it does not - more of the latter. Oh we can muscle through things, some may do it very well. We can even fake our way through techniques by always using strength - some may never know the difference. But there is a difference and you should know what it is. The use of strength is something that wears us down, tires us out, increases our breathing and slows our movements. When we use strength, we can never really be in total control of the technique, let alone uke. Since our concentration is on out muscling our opponent, we forget about our own center, our own balance, uke's center and balance, even the technique itself. Just because we have gripped uke's wrist with "grip of steel" and are applying the "grasp of death", does not mean we control uke - maybe their wrist but not the body - or more importantly their center.

Using proper technique is a chore for us all. But applied correctly, technique affords us the time to stay in control and assess the situation. It opens our eyes to holes in uke's defenses and makes us aware of what is around us. When we make the decision to use strength, uke feels this and responds with the same. Now it becomes a contest and Aikido is not about competition it is about mutual harmony.

Strength has never been equated to an intelligent, tactical response. Timing, speed, relaxation and good technique are elements that make one up. Train as if you are weak in muscle but strong in spirit and technique will shine through always.

When All Else Fails
After you have given muscling the technique a try and long after all the herky, jerky sensations your uke has experienced on your account, and after you have tugged and pulled at your partner's arm, you may want to try and apply some of the principles that make an Aikido movement work efficiently. We all need to get it out of our systems. For some it may take longer than others. Some may never break the chains. Thus, uke is left to endure the hardships of strength-based nage techniques.

We are all guilty of this situation at one time or another. Sometimes it seems like the only way to get through a technique. It can be very frustrating for everyone and in the grand scheme, does not lend to proper learning. The first thing we need to do is to become aware that we are doing it. Try to relax before beginning a technique – take a deep breath and focus. Work on one thing at a time. Move at a slow but steady and controlled pace. This will allow for total focus, thus, being aware of what we are doing. If we run into a section where the technique seems to lack the power we need take the opportunity and find out why. Plowing through with everything you have is not the answer. And your uke may not be very receptive to work with you in the future. And sometimes, on uke's end, you give what you get. If you are not sure, ask Sensei. Your instructor is there to help. Taking the time to work through it is the best remedy to better learning and better performance.

So when all else fails – try doing the technique with technique!

In life, we give up control if we are always forcing the situation. We lose sight of the bigger picture. Less is better and it is the subtle things that make the big difference.

Points on a Sphere

During aiki movement we occupy many different positions. If we look at our movement as working within a personal sphere, we contact numerous positional points on that sphere. At times we are at the center and uke is at the outer edge. Other times uke is at the center and nage occupies the outer edge. And there are times when uke and nage are at the outer edge and the lead of technique resides at the center. Aikido will reveal these points if we remain open and aware.

A sphere is a three-dimensional object that is symmetrically designed having all points equidistant from their center. No matter where the point, it leads to and from center. This is a great example of a core element in Aikido – center is at the heart of our being. The sphere has no boundaries and is able to join together with other objects during movement. The use of our space in Aikido resembles the same and with it we are able to expand and contract the size of our sphere depending on our needs. So, within our personal sphere, we are capable of an infinite series and infinite paths of movement in motion.

Advancing in Shape

Movement can take on many path shapes. In Aikido we primarily speak of the triangle, circle and square. The triangle represents irimi, our entering either offensively or defensively. The circle represents our transitional movements, where uke's balance or kuzushi is broken (taken). The square represents the line of execution or kake of technique. Together, these shapes and what they represent create one powerful movement.

Triangle

The triangle is considered the strongest of all shapes. In its 3D form – a pyramid – the triangle is impenetrable. In movement the triangle has two distinct functions: offense and defense. It dictates direction, position, provides protection, offers a line of offense and defense and creates or closes openings. When we are attacked we have two options: 1) move and counter to the outside or 2) move and counter to the inside - regardless if we step in or step back.

Moving and countering to the outside takes on a more defensive position. Our movement cancels the attacker's weapons, positions us outside or behind the line of fire and our attacker's sights – we enter from the angel at 45 degrees.

Moving and countering to the inside takes on a more offensive position. We enter towards the attacker's centerline and inside the attack – where the corner point of the triangle enters first along the centerline.

In both positions we can gain a great advantage.

Moving to the outside of an attack creates the fastest means of our escape. It places all of our attacker's weapons to one side – this creates a controlled environment for us. In one move we have boxed in our opponent and gained the upper hand. We must then decide to make our escape or set in motion a series of defenses, through an array of strikes, controlling tactics and takedowns that will subdue our attacker and their efforts.

Moving to the inside of the attack puts us right into the action – some believe this is the safest place to be – like in the eye of the storm. We are keyed into our attacker's frontal centerline, giving us numerous choices of targets- all at a very close range. This affords us quick and accurate connections.

Circle
The circle represents the continuous flow that evolves within technique and in turn, evolving from within us. The circle is the transitional path Aikido uses to redirect and generate enormous amounts of power. There is no end – no end to the movement, no end to the power it can create, no end to its possibilities. Its use allows us to function in the smallest of areas or in the largest of spaces. The path it defines leads both inward and outward – all depending on our needs. In part or in whole, with the use of the circle's design we are able to move mountains or simply displace our partner's stability to create ease of execution. Our use of the circle is defined by the role we play – are we the center of the circle and uke and technique are the outer edges, or is it that we share the outer edge with uke and the technique in its purest form is the center? The choice is ours.

There are two general circular paths – horizontal and vertical; horizontal to transition and break uke's balance and vertical to execute a throw. A conventional circle, however, is not always the common path. We may take obscure circular paths such as an oval or ellipse, to achieve our goal - moving in and out and up and down. But whatever the design, we are harnessing the power created within a circular path.

When we begin to break down our movements we find that these circular paths make movement more efficient with minimal effort and it maximizes our power of execution. At times these paths can create motion or energy where there is little or none, as is the case with static grabs. Knowledge of these paths and their usefulness will increase an Aikido-ka's skill and proficiency at any level.

Square

The square then represents our final line of execution. Where the triangle has created our entry, and the circle has enhanced our power, the square provides the path to make it all come together. Execution or kake of technique flows on this path. Kake is where we have come to commit our resolution with our partner. Execution encompasses all of what we have set out to do. Kake is our final solution. The path of the square embodies the end result of the total package. The quickest route between two points is a straight line.

Without its counterparts, the triangle and the circle, the square is incomplete. It is just part of a whole. One feeds the next – from beginning to end. One cannot stand alone and be truly effective. It is through the unity of the three that technique is derived. Through this unity we come to grow as true Aikido-ka, in mind, body and spirit.

Essential Movement

Regardless of our choice of movement, we must work towards an immediate escape to safety. If we must engage, through atemi (strikes), locks, etc., keep it to a minimum until escape is possible. The longer we are in the mix, the greater our chances of being overcome and we run the risk of serious injury or far worse.

To achieve our escape constant movement is the key. If we stay in one place too long we become that place. Keep moving and become a hard target. The movement will open options of escape and decrease the chances of being hit.

When we are one with the movement we are one with the universe for that period of time - for an instant – that is when we generate the most power.

True honest movement is not swayed or influenced except by other movement.

An object in motion tends to stay in motion especially when amplified by other motion – when connected the motion intensifies.

Motion creates opportunity for off balance – both in uke and nage.

Movement is movement – it is pure. The intent makes movement offensive or defensive, positive or negative.

Movement is essential for survival. Our mindset should not be the defeat of our attacker. Our mindset must be our immediate safety. Safety comes first. This is not ego – this is survival. So when you're opening comes – take it and run.

No one can determine the outcome of any event. It is not ours to decide. Consistent training can better your odds. Repetitive drilling of movement exercises will condition our natural response. We want it to just happen – when we see movement – we respond with movement, and with each movement, we place ourselves out of harm's way until an escape is created.

How does constant movement pertain to everyday non-life threatening situations? If we work to stay in constant motion, in thought, in action, in intent, we will never be subject to the mundane. Our constant motion creates an energy, a positive force that will radiate to those around us. This positive energy can diffuse possible negative elements that may cross our path and halt our forward progression. Our constant state of movement sends out a

signal that we are moving forward, that we will make the
best of any situation or circumstance, that regardless of what stands
before us we will emerge victorious.

Movement is energy in motion and the more movement we do the
more energy we create, the more energy we will have to withstand
life's ups and downs. The more energy we generate we run the risk
of passing that energy on to another, who passes it on to another and
so on. Until one day the world is a complete ball of positive energy
in constant motion.

*Movement is energy in motion, the more
movement we do the more energy we create...*

V. Roles
- Uke/Nage

Being Uke - Being Nage

Uke/nage have specific roles for technique to function properly - each having roles to learn and roles to fulfill for true learning to take place. These roles function as a means to incorporate efficient body mechanics and center aligning and aids in maintaining maximum power without overtaxing our resources. Without an understanding and discipline to learn these roles we can never truly embrace the art. Remembering our role lends to a better learning environment for all.

Uke and nage's relationship is based in technique. We are executing a specific response to a specific action. The scenario practiced is built from a small segment of a confrontation - part of a possibly greater encounter. This scenario training teaches us the basic outline of what is entailed in developing a conditioned response.

Ukemi, by basic design, is the receiving of technique or movement through movement. Ukemi can be performed by both uke and nage.

In either role we must commit to receive what is given – this is the main role – the way of the art.

Movement, in itself, is technique in the simplest form regardless of the role one receives or chooses. Without it, we become sitting targets, hence we learn nothing. Receiving technique or receiving movement imparts an ability to read the intent or feel the actions of our partner. Receiving technique is not simply allowing our partners to apply a defense then we respond; whereas our ukemi is conditioned only after pain or injury has been received. Rather, it is the development of a sense of awareness that allows us to adapt to these movements and respond accordingly - to defend or protect ourselves against pain or injury. Our movements then become an extension of our partner's movements. These movements can be martial and/or artistic in their approach and execution. For example, if uke pushes, nage pulls or turns. If uke pulls, nage enters and pushes.

The Uke Role

Uke receives a technique from nage through ukemi.

Uke takes time to learn what ukemi is, how to perform ukemi and what ukemi can do for them. The use of solo training and partner drills will greatly enhance the ukemi experience and understanding.

To be uke means we must take ukemi to blend with the movement or technique. To deal with movement or technique properly we must accept it fully.

Ukemi should not be looked at as only falling. There are several levels of ukemi and falling is but one. Ukemi can be broken down into three categories - responsive, defensive or offensive.

Responsive ukemi is when technique is executed and your body responds – falling from an applied joint lock or from a strike to the face or simply from loss of balance

Defensive ukemi is an escape through falling or blending with the movement – keeping enough distance between uke and nage affording an opportunity to escape.

Offensive ukemi creates an opening to counter by blending. We can find openings in our partner if we are sensitive to their movements.

When we attack as uke we must stay with the line of attack – keeping our center and continuously moving towards nage's center; but keeping proper distance with our weapon – not leading with our head or feet - and always driving the motion with our center. We need to commit to the attack – not just the movement but also the intent of attack. We need to keep nage in our sights and move to keep the centers aligned. If we attack off center (i.e. body center is in one direction and the attack or weapon is in another) we never generate enough power and end up relying solely on strength.

Being uke is being aware of what is going on; with ourselves, with our partner and with our surroundings. Movement dictates movement. True honest movement dictates movement – not the person.

Movement is an action reaction response. Ukemi relates to nage's directional lead not to uke's directional pull. If uke has time to pull, then there was never a committed attack from uke or nage did not initiate a lead for uke to follow.

As uke, during ukemi, commit to connect with nage but do not become the attack. If we do become the attack we become uncentered, unbalanced and out of control. Again drive the attack with your body, from your center and maintain proper distance. Proper distance will allow your ukemi to pull you through. Do not attempt to control the ukemi but rather control yourself doing ukemi.

Uke needs to accept and embrace this connection. Again we must be sensitive enough to rely on the feel of the movement to find the path of escape or to show the opening in our partner's defense.

The Nage Role
Nage means to throw. Nage makes connections with uke's movement. Nage's connection with the movement initiated by uke puts nage in control. This control creates a choice to stay with it or go around it. If we stay with it our options are to direct the movement in its original direction or redirect the movement someplace else. Movement achieves control or lead. Not opposing movement but blending, flowing movement.

As nage we need to connect with uke but not become uke - one with uke's movement not uke the person. Nage then takes the lead and controls the movement. Nage will also need to be sensitive enough to feel what uke is doing in the event that timing and lead are lost. To regain our lead we must continue to follow the movement that is created or amplified.

Nage must learn control. How much do I give? How much is necessary to control the situation? Again this comes down to learning to feel. This is why we speak of using the whole body and mind connection. It is not about making impact and causing injury. It is about preserving life and blending with it.

Uke and nage's intent needs to be that of commitment. Commit to each role and the relationship based in technique will build out of trust.

Both uke and nage are responsible for themselves as well as each other. It is nage's responsibility to realize the level of uke, and if you don't know it, ask uke if they're comfortable with a move, or a fall. If nage doesn't ask, it's uke's responsibility to let nage know his/her limitations and comfort levels. You are both there to help each other learn...realize that and use it to your learning advantage.

Sometimes when we work with each other, we tend to rush through a technique and miss the subtle nuances that make the move effective. It is a good idea to work a move slowly at first until both nage and uke get used to each other and the move, before bringing up the intensity. In doing this, we learn to take responsibility for our own actions; we can increase confidence in ourselves and in our partners and also decrease the chance of injury.

Our roles as humans in the everyday world are not that different. We are responsible for our actions. Though we are not responsible for the actions of others, we must take responsibility to inform others of their actions and present to them what is appropriate in how they treat us. What we say and how we act can have a greater impact on the lives and decisions of others then if we just sit and watch the train go by. This is also true of how we treat ourselves. Our true responsibility is to a greater, safer, more harmonious world. We can achieve this by one positive action at a time.

How We Train
At times we train hard - pushing the limits of our throwing power and our ability for big break falls. Other times we train fast - building speed and timing. And still other times we train waza – slowly executing the movements to gain insight and accuracy. We do this to get better - to reach the next level and begin again. We do this for our partner and ourselves.

Training can be one sided - meaning that our partner does not have the same intent as we do. Their attack may not be committed, they might pull after they have given, they resist and dictate how, when and where they ukemi. This is frustrating and does not help at all with both parties' learning. The principles of Aikido technique are based on movement, not just nage's movement but the movement of uke as well. It is easy for uke to say, "I know what is coming so

I can make the technique not work", or "I do not like that fall so I will resist or fall how I want to fall". In these cases, nothing is gained for either practitioner. Sure we know what is coming, it's practice, but Aikido is based on movements relating the intent through attack. Without movement there is no attack; therefore, no need for a defense. Sure we know what is coming, what we don't know is when it is coming. That makes it exciting. That makes it real. Intent plays a crucial role in learning Aikido not only as nage but more so for uke. Attacking with intent means that you have entrusted your partner as well as yourself from the moment you engage to the

Our true responsibility is to a greater,
safer, more harmonious world.

moment you hit the mat. We trust that nage will move out of the way with proper timing and speed. We trust that nage will continue our movement by extending the lead. And we trust that nage will throw us with the energy that we as uke have committed to them.

Nage, in turn, trusts uke to have the intent to fully attack, to not pull back or resist because of a half-hearted attempt. Most importantly, nage trusts that uke will provide proper ukemi for their efforts without hesitation and without fail.

If there is a fear of falling, make it known and work through it. Once it is made known, we must trust nage to throw us in a manner becoming our current level of understanding and performance. Again it is easy to say as uke "I can get out of this because I know what is coming". But in real life when we are attacked, our attacker does not know what is coming. All they know is that they are attacking - hard and fast with intent. So to defend we must move, blend with that oncoming energy, redirect it and subdue it. To not have intent in the dojo is misleading to your training and a viable learning tool to forego. This is not to say that our intent is to hurt, punish or destroy our partner. Rather an attack must be made with intent to learn and to help others learn. We learn with the help of one another. Without each other we train warding off shadows. Shadows are not dangerous.

In life, creating trust in our relationships only enhances the experience. It creates a bond and builds character. It teaches us to think of others and not only of ourselves. It shows us that the needs of the many outweigh the needs of the one. Trust is a sacred connection in training; it is priceless. Trust in yourself to trust in others. Show trust and you will be trusted.

We learn with the help of one another.

In life, creating trust in our relationships only enhances the experience.

VI. Parts of a Throw
- Entry, Off-balance and Execution

Irimi – Entering In
In almost every encounter, evasion is a large percentage of the battle. If we move out of the line of a strike we have allowed ourselves time to defend and counter or escape. Irimi, entering and yoke, evasion, are an Aikido-ka's first lines of defense. Irimi places us within or just outside uke's attack. It will not matter how many techniques you know if you stand there and are hit or injured. By getting out of the way we gain another second. Irimi happens in a blink of an eye. Irimi movement can follow the cadence of nage's breathing or uke's breathing. Thus timing plays a major role in our ability to get out of the way. Techniques can be enhanced through daily practice of basic movements. We will engrain our response and our response time as normal movement. By breaking our movements down and dissecting what is irimi, we will be able to concentrate on our timing and develop the necessary skills to achieve the power of entering. In time we will find that our reactions are quicker, giving us more time for our defense.

Kuzushi – The Taking of Balance
The taking of uke's balance can be looked at as the most essential moment of any technique once we have entered properly. It is this crucial point that determines how the rest of the technique will proceed. The taking of balance, kuzushi, ensures nage's success and allows us to execute with maximum efficiency. Without this, our attempts rely solely on strength and in many cases we may instead lose our own balance in the process. Often kuzushi can occur at the same point of entry - whether that entry is for evasion or follow up. Uke must believe that their target is where they see it and commit to the attack. As they do, nage moves offline and enters. This entering has uke committing to empty space and causes uke to be off balance. Off balance occurs when uke's center has shifted weight, either to their heels or toes. This is nage's job, to make the shift of uke's weight by using uke's committed energy. Off balance does not occur just because we have made uke twist or bend at the waist. We must make the shift of uke's center to give us full advantage. Once achieved, what comes next is up to nage's imagination.

Kake – Execution

The climax of technique, the point where all of our efforts are given the time to shine, is kake, the execution. With the proper, effective application of the prior steps, irimi and kuzushi, execution should be effortless. Kake is the time to throw uke, dissipating any possible threat, while maintaining a level of harmony between the two. Our goal in execution is to control the situation to a degree that no one involved is harmed. Because nage has employed proper irimi, proper kuzushi, following through with effortless kake, degrees of control can be achieved. These degrees of control result in nage's ability to determine the severity of the situation - only giving as much as is needed to maintain mutual harmony.

Execution is the result of a harmonious intent on the part of nage. So, the intent to damage or destroy will result in such. If this is our intent, we must intend to take responsibility for what happens next. With an intent on maintaining peace and personal safety – which includes the safety of others - we will do only what is necessary to achieve that state, no more.

Center It

The one constant during any technique, it is the undisputable fact that we must move from and with our center. Without this we fall short of exuding our ultimate power and extension by being off balance and resorting to muscle strength and clumsiness. Our center is a point in which we become "one with the universe" - a place where everything is in perfect harmony. Of course this is an idea easier said than done, but is a cornerstone in the Aikido experience. Moving from center has been described as having a rubber band attached just below your mid-section and as you move the constant tension pulls you forward, generating power. Posture is enhanced once we allow our center to control our movements. Bad posture is evident in the Aikido-ka that has allowed their head or feet to lead the technique, or in the case where we loose balance during execution. This losing of balance is due to lack of center. Without center we allow ourselves as nage or uke to be easily overpowered and out-maneuvered. Think of your center as the center of the earth's core. It expels heat in all directions equally. Our movements should do the same when we properly enable our centers. Thus, to achieve perfect center we must achieve a state of focus.

Focus

One of the hardest things to do in any circumstance is getting focused and staying focused. At times on the mat we fumble through technique. While trying to remember to extend, to keep proper posture, to blend, to breathe and so on, we may get frustrated and begin to lose whatever amount of focus we may have started with. When we seem to reach these points in training, more times than we would like to admit, we must first realize that it is happening and stop, take a step back and breathe. We need to decipher what we are doing and what we may be doing incorrectly. We then need to break down the exercise and work it one step at a time until we have achieved personal satisfactory results. When we become aware of these "momentary periods of confusion", we will be able to stop it before it completely allows us to lose focus.

While executing our techniques, we should maintain an awareness of our surroundings - people, places and things. What might become confusing and possibly counterproductive is that if we are watching our surroundings, we may become distracted and lose site of our immediate threat - our attacker.

Being aware of our surroundings in times of dangerous situations is important and effective, making ourselves aware of future threats. But to be efficient we must face one situation at a time. The present situation holds precedence to future ones and must be dealt with as such. We are instructed not to watch our hands or the attack of our uke. These actions could cause us to momentarily freeze up and react late, inhibiting a proper response. Instead watch our partner as a whole, focusing on the centerline, allowing us to develop a stronger set of focal points in our defense, both current and future. Without focusing on one particular thing we can be focused on everything all at once. We can see and feel our partner's actions, counters or resistance while staying in touch with our surroundings.

Attacking the Center

Attack seems like such a harsh word to be using in Aikido training. To attack anything is contradictory to the ideology and philosophies that Aikido teaches. But if we look at the attack as something that is set in motion during our defensive measures it may not seem as harsh.

Initial movement for nage in Aikido consists of moving out of the way, and capturing the center of our uke. Capturing center means to take the balance of uke in a way that our own movement is not hindered or balance altered and now controls the movements of our partner. While entering, irimi, we must place ourselves within the oncoming energy before uke's advance ever reaches us - like entering the eye of the storm. By "attacking the center" we position ourselves in a stable and controlled environment. We have entered the center of the circle. This extension to uke's center places them off balance and diffuses the power of their attack. Uke's weapons are now compromised. Nage has created time to respond. Through this focused approach nage is then able to control the situation.

By attacking uke's center, we may end the conflict before it has a chance to gain real momentum. This can be practiced during our irimi movement. As we enter, extend into the technique by leading our movement with tegatana - hand blade. This extension creates a constant; it creates a predetermined space between uke and nage. Driven by our entire body movement while directed towards uke's center, nage will make not only a physical connection before uke, but a mental one as well, diffusing the attack and capturing the energy.

Defense Science
We all have been overwhelmed at times when dealing with techniques. We worry about what step follows what move and what are the placement of our hands, feet and so on. We rush through movements, to gain speed, using muscle or we do the hard parts slow and the easier parts fast, never setting a consistent flow.
Our execution becomes choppy or robotic because all we did was memorize a sequence of movements. What's lost is the essence of feeling and flow, the true nature of what the technique is designed to accomplish and what it is attempting to teach us. Break things down in the learning process. Everything should be practiced at the same pace including uke's attacks. We need to digest not only the sequence of movements but also learning the feel and timing of each. Working together and repetitive training will reinforce this concept.

The most important part that we often neglect is the initial blending – a real and constant connection. If we blend, we give ourselves plenty of time to flow and feel. Much of what we do is body mechanics and simple physics. We are not performing magic or illusions. Each action propagates an equal and opposite reaction. It is these reactions that we use in our techniques when defending ourselves. There is also a part that involves allowing ourselves to respond as things unveil. Sometimes technique does not happen by the book and we can find ourselves just doing. We deal with each moment as it comes, feeling and flowing our way through.

Just allow it to unfold and embrace the opportunities to work out these concepts. Learn what to do, but feel how it's done. Timing and speed are the benefits and will come once we are comfortable with the movements and ourselves.

VII. Intentions

Intent is what motivates all we do. Intent is what motivates conflict. And conflict is motivated by fear. For an attacker, it is the intent to harm another. For the defender, it is the intent to protect what is precious to them – quality of life.

So to effectively defend we must understand the intent of the attacker. Intent is most dangerous when acted upon. It is one thing to say something harmful but another level to act on it.

Martial ways were designed to preserve life in troubled times. These ways were also a means to develop and care for the inner self. They are but a path to enhance life – not to take it; to respect life – not dishonor it.

Aikido is not a solo martial art. It involves levels of communications with others – physical, mental, emotional and spiritual.

We must train not only our bodies but our minds as well. We must educate ourselves just as we would for anything else. Create a better understanding and we will broaden the tools necessary to respond. Aikido is the tool of understanding.

What's in your Heart?
When you come to train at the dojo – consider why are you there. Is it solely for your own benefit? Is working with others, helping them achieve their goals, something that fulfills you?

Aikido helps in cultivating relationships. These relationships can build a better community while building a better you. The opportunity to help another is a gift that benefits all. We can learn so much by giving so little – our time and our attention. Sometimes just a few words of encouragement to a fellow student can make a huge difference in how they see themselves or how they perform. Simple direction or insight that allows them to enhance their training can be a turning point. Aikido is not a solo martial art. It involves levels of communications with others – physical, mental, emotional and spiritual. By words or actions these levels can be reached – both positively and negatively.

Aikido lays out many challenges before the practitioner. Many seem unobtainable at first. With time, practice and the support of your fellow Aikido-ka these challenges are met. No one reaches these levels by themselves. Everyone along the way has contributed somehow in your growth and understanding. We share the mat as a network of support. We strive for the greater good. We face these challenges together.

The challenges we face are not easy ones. But together there is strength in numbers. Because to face a challenge alone can be daunting rather with others it becomes encouraging. If we cannot give of ourselves then we can never expect to truly receive the gifts that will make us whole – compassion, mercy and love.

Aikido is a way of finding your purpose in life. This purpose involves others. When you give to another, that person will give to another and so on and so on. The cycle will continue, thus, creating a better community, a better world – one based in harmony with one another.

Next time you come to train, ask yourself "Why am I here?" and "What can I do for another?" Really see what is in your heart.

Intent to Learn
In the beginning, to properly perform a technique, we must have total cooperation from our partner. This does not say that the techniques do not work. It is saying that we care enough for the other person and their learning. How will they know what to do if not given the opportunity to do? In return they do the same for us. Our intent to learn and to help learn is based on our commitment to the process. This means being patient - with others and ourselves.

Be understanding - we all struggle with learning.

Be respectful - to others, the dojo and yourself.

Be cooperative - committing to attacks and to the movement as both uke and nage.

It is easy to hurt others. We do not need martial arts training for this. So what would we really gain from hurting another? Where does it put us? Helping others progress is a true test of character and benefits all involved. We gain the satisfaction of knowing we were there for another - that we played a role in their progression. Together we learn and together we grow - this is Aikido.

Realism

Are you looking for a resistant realism, where you leave the dojo angry, with cuts, bruises and/or serious injuries, which may also prevent you from tending to your life's responsibilities and possibly future classes?

Or are you looking for a cooperative realism, where there is a committed attack that extends with energy for nage to blend with, where full extension can be incorporated knowing that your partner can defend themselves with proper ukemi and where mutual harmony is the collective goal?

In the cooperative realism, the attacks are real in the sense that if your timing is off you get hit. There is an element of surprise that occurs, where reaction takes precedence to action, where an attack is fast and hard, where we do not have time to think, but rather, respond. We may know what technique is coming we just may not know when it is coming.

Many of us confuse resistance to or resistance in an attack as a well-executed committed attack. If there is resistance in an initial attack then there is no real attack, no threat. Resistance occurs after an attacker realizes his/her efforts have become useless and begins alternate measures. The Aikido-ka, (nage, in this case) whose timing and techniques have been well executed to a legitimate attack, will not experience resistance. The attacker would be unaware of nage's intentions when his/her attack commenced; thus, the element of surprise.

Resistance is far too common in the dojo because uke knows what's coming. Often, attacks are not committed or uke may fight a technique. When this occurs, both uke and nage fail to learn the technique.

Then what is realism? Is it practicing squaring off with one another to see who will remain standing? This may be realism, but it is not practical. What is gained in allowing uke and nage to beat on one another? What would the point be in studying Aikido or any martial art? One could walk the streets and pick fights with the locals to hone in on that type of skill. Aikido is more!

Aikido studies are a sophisticated, ethical approach to preserve life with minimal harm to another and oneself. This is not to say we allow ourselves to be thrown – but as uke, it is essential that we commit ourselves to our attacks and fully and openly take responsibility for those attacks to expect a committed reaction from nage and perform proper ukemi on our part. This way everyone learns, everyone reaps the benefits.

合気道

Aikido

Challenge Yourself

During our lifetime of training, we need to become aware of what our comfort levels are and work on challenging them. Comfort levels are what we emotionally, mentally, physically and spiritually will not go beyond when something or someone alters our normal course of doing. Comfort levels prevent us from learning and growing. It is when we feel most comfortable that we must push ourselves to the next level as long as it is not life threatening. Easier said then done I assure you, but possible and in the end, very beneficial.

Doing what is comfortable is easy but in the process we learn nothing and never grow. Challenging ourselves to move to the next level, to take another step or to incorporate a new set of ideas are what brings about great feats of change and growth. Next time you are on the mat challenge yourself even in the smallest way.

Self challenge is an individual thing. Each person has a different set of goals that they strive to achieve. Setting goals is a challenge in and of itself. Working towards attaining those goals sets us apart.

Self challenge has to do with each of us going beyond what we know to be comfortable and venture into an area of discomfort and sacrifice. Sacrifice the same old easy route for a vastly beneficial challenging one – here is where true and lasting self-growth takes place. Keep in mind that the end result is a stronger better you.

Challenge yourself everyday.

We all learn a system or an art. But the style
that one demonstrates comes from within.

合氣道

VIII. Individualize
- Make it your Own

Often, practitioners question why we do certain things and why these certain things do not seem to work for them when they just watched it demonstrated. Whereas it may be a case of strengthening the basics, there will come times when what is prescribed as a means to employ technique may not work in our reality. This may lead to frustration and confusion for any level of student.

Regardless of art or system we all learn concepts – concepts for action/reaction situations. All have their methods though at times these concepts we learn as a whole do not seem to be the method of choice for certain students to confront a particular attack. Often students are given only one view and little guidance or encouragement, if offered at all, to further explain the movement and ease their confusion. As students and instructors we need to take from these concepts certain ideas and approaches and apply them to our individual movements and thought process. Once the basics are grasped and a certain level of proficiency is achieved, it becomes the responsibility of the practitioner, indifferent of level, to enhance personal technique by incorporating these personal approaches. As instructors, it is our responsibility to the student, to the art/system, to find that personal attribute in them and allow it to shine through in their execution. Use that strength to build on, furthering the student's understanding and confidence level.

There are many techniques, many ways these techniques are demonstrated, many ways to perform them and many people who aspire to learn them. To say one technique approach is right and another approach is wrong is close-minded. Techniques come in all shapes and sizes, as do the people who perform them. The best technique is the best approach that suits the individual performing them. We all must achieve a constant performance of basic form and posture, rudimentary rules for off balance and control. Once there is a grasp of these concepts, we must take this knowledge and ascertain the correct execution for ourselves. "*To break the rules is to know the rules*". The person demonstrating the technique might be taller, larger build, be able to cover greater ground with only a few steps or may be even smaller in stature allowing for easy access with a lower center of gravity.

At times we struggle with techniques because we are seeing one person do it in a particular way, and in many cases those individuals have already integrated their personal interpretation of that technique to their own attributes of execution. They do what works for them. That is what many of us need to do to reach higher levels, both in understanding and execution.

We all learn a system or an art. But the style that one demonstrates comes from within. What may be taken for granted in many arts/ systems is that there is more then one way to achieve the same goal. There are countless approaches to a single technique and everyone needs to be open to this for true internal and external growth. This is what makes the martial arts exciting. Still, we all must possess the basic skill level needed to complete the techniques, but nuances in steps, stances, body shifts, etc, all become an individual's style of interpretation, hence walking their individual path.

Take what we know about the techniques and ourselves - take what the instructor demonstrates and adapt that to what you are capable of doing. Attempt to move toward a better understanding of what you have to offer to the technique by focusing on your strengths. By doing so your lesser qualities will begin to improve. This approach is a never-ending process since we will always be changing, both in thought and skill level. As we become more in tune with our abilities, the better our techniques will become and the better we will become.

Individual Paths
When we begin training in Aikido, we are very excited and gung ho. As time progresses some of us begin to feel lost, confused or even frustrated and toy with the idea of quitting. These are trying times and with some more disciplined practice one can overcome and reach new plateaus.

Art is something that is individual - something that grows and continues to grow and evolve as one devotes their time to it. The longer you are involved, the more ways you find to express yourself. What gets one man thinking or doing does not always make another do the same. We all must have a strong foundation - a base to grow from - this is why the basic movements are hammered home. But in time we must all find our own path - our own way of understanding.

Own Your Training

For many of us our martial arts training is a scheduled day, at a particular location, for a set period of time. Once the training session has been completed our martial arts training - or better yet, education - is put back on the shelf until the next scheduled session. This is the way our lives have become, not only with the arts, but also with all that we do. Life is a series of schedules and time frames.

To truly evolve and prosper in the martial arts we must take ownership of our training. We need to become responsible for the courage to begin. We must exude the patience to learn. We must desire the discipline to succeed. The key is the discipline – self-discipline.

This self-discipline is the true test of ownership for ones words, thoughts and actions. Without it we are just going through the motions. It is easy to make a decision but to stick with it and develop it, care for it and build on it, nurture it and be accountable for it – this is the difficult part – this is self-discipline.

To fully promote our personal growth in the martial arts, we must make no excuses, give no IOUs and must not offer ourselves a reason to fail. If you think you can – you can. If you think you cannot – then you will not.

The same holds true in daily life. We must take responsibility for our words and actions and the possible consequences associated with them – good and bad. We must learn to be aware of the needs of others and act when called upon to do our part in creating a better world. At times fulfilling the needs of others fulfills a need in us. We can discover a whole new world of being. And the joy we experience by being there for another.

Aikido training teaches us a relationship built on harmony and mutual benefit is a strong and lasting one. When you are strong enough to trust another then another will be strong enough to trust in you.

Have You Found Your Own Individual Path?
We are all drawn to something – something that intrigues us,
captivates us, motivates and inspires us. It is that special something
that makes getting out of bed worth doing - that certain something
that washes away all the clutter in our daily routines. We make great
efforts to engage in that special something whenever we can. That
special something can make the difference in how we feel, how we
act, how we think, and how we relate to others.

For those of us at the dojo, Aikido is that special something. And with
it brings the individuals' needs to find their own way. Aikido sets
us on a path but it does not tell us which way to go. Aikido gives us
direction but it is the student who chooses the road. Some will choose
a physical one while others a spiritual endeavor. Some dwell in both.
Some will attempt to imitate those who came before and some will
venture to stand on their own. Many will find the path too difficult
and a few will press on as the road becomes more challenging.

Aikido offers us a foundation to build upon - a foundation that
transcends from the training mat and into everyday life. "Aikido is
but a stone thrown into a pond. We – the students – are the ripples".
Each ripple makes its own way out. Aikido is our center, but the
road we take is our own individual path.

Walk your individual path and you may find that you light the way
for others to do the same.

IX. Working in the Now

In the Now

"Naka ima" is Japanese for "inside now" or "in the now". For the Aikido-ka in the dojo, it relates to how we face technique. This is a state of mind. When we approach a technique, familiar or new, we can concern ourselves with overall performance rather than technique. Just doing the movement alone is not technique. No thought is placed on what is happening. Nage may be worried about how the technique is to finish and does not have their mind on the steps in between. But without these steps we would be unable to execute the final move in the technique. With this in mind, we must be in the moment each step of the way. Being in the now as it is happening, not allowing ourselves to get caught up in the past or the future. Each movement in the technique creates the next. The past is gone and the future has an infinite amount of possibilities. It is this one particular moment, which will define what follows.

We must allow ourselves when in practice to slow down and analyze what we are doing, what we are trying to achieve. Hence working in the now: *naka ima*.

Time In – Time Out – Time Spent

What do you want from your training? What is it that keeps you coming consistently to class or not so consistently to class?

This is an important question. Without the answer we do not have a goal or direction to focus on. If the answer is simply to learn the martial arts we may need to take the time a find a deeper meaning. To learn the martial arts is saying that you begin this life long journey of self discovery and intend to explore every known and unknown facet of it without allowing the world and all its detours to get in your way. Does that sound right? We need to give ourselves specific and detailed goals to focus on one at a time. This can never be achieved if we choose not to attend classes and train - to train on the days even when we do not feel like it, when things just keep going wrong, when you do not know your left from your right, when there is better things to do or when the weather is just right. These are the days we must train and train hard. Each day we train is one step closer to attaining our goal. If we allow ourselves to fall short of our own goals we can never achieve self mastery in anything we do.

Time in or time out, either way it is time spent. You decide how you spend your time. Somewhere down the line you made the decision to study a martial art. You chose Aikido. Now it is up to you, for yourself, to make good on that decision and spend your time wisely. We cannot gain what we do not go to get. Decide what you want to get out of it and once you have decided that, decide what you are willing to put into it to get out what you want. It is a balance.

The same decision is what we must make on a daily basis. What is it we want out of life, out of the day before us, out of the people around us and out of ourselves? The possibilities are endless. The choice you make may have an impact on who you are so real and lasting change can occur. It must pertain to your total package – your higher self and the higher good. How we live or choose not to live defines who we are. Will you live with vigor and passion? Or will your days be spent wallowing in self-doubt and pity?

To get what we desire, we must give over and over again. Giving to others gives back to us on so many levels.

Value what you do, the choices you make, the people around you. Most importantly value who you are and what you will become.

Value It

Value in life seems to be a consistent theme for many of us. What value we get for the money we spend or the time we invest. Products and services are built on the notion that if we own it or use it we add value to our lives. But is it really valuable? Something can only be valuable if we truly value it. If not, it is just adding more clutter into our lives.

We need to discern what constitutes value - our families, friends, our job or careers, how we spend our time and what we fill our days with, better yet what we fill our thoughts and hearts with. What we determine to be of value should not be swayed by advertising and marketing campaigns but rather by how it helps us grow and become a better individual. How does it affect our lives and how does it cause us to affect the lives of those around us?

Focus on the moment. In Japanese, moment is setsuna, a poetic use of the word signifying living in the moment or instant. Setsuna asks us to make each moment we live count not just for us but for everything and everyone – use each moment, each "instant" to make a positive lasting effect on the world. Only you can value its importance, its pure power valuing who we are and what we can become. With value comes the responsibility to be true to it – to inevitably being true to you.

Value what you do, the choices you make, the people around you. Most importantly value who you are and what you will become.

X. Ukemi
- The Art of Falling

The Right Uke - Realism in Ukemi

During our training we may be faced with an immovable uke - one who is seemingly impossible to work with: an uncooperative uke. While we struggle to perform, we may feel as though our technique is insufficient, or missing something that the instructor had demonstrated. Even the most experienced veteran has moments when they questioned their abilities.

Now to some the statement of being cooperative may imply that Aikido is fake and our partner is taking a fall. But Aikido is the blending of energy. How can one blend when there is no energy? If there is no energy, there is no threat. And if there is no threat we are able to walk away. Many people believe by cooperating as uke they are giving something up of themselves. Ego may play a large role in others who are not cooperative. These same people expect in their uke what they are not giving. In fact, to properly train, both uke and nage must fully commit. This way nage is capable of executing at full intensity all the while knowing uke is performing quality ukemi without the fear of serious injury.

Ukemi is three-fold. First, it is a means of receiving an attack. Our bodies are taught to feel the movement and intentions of our partner and conditioned to respond appropriately to alleviate the possibility of serious injury.

Second, ukemi is a means of escape – breaking free of a joint lock or creating distance between our partner and us.

And third, ukemi is a means of taking a fall – one that is initiated voluntarily or involuntarily.

Ukemi is an art in itself and requires dedicated training. How can we perform ukemi if we are reluctant to practice taking ukemi?

Often we may neglect to realize that if attacked for real, outside the dojo, the majority of attackers will not react to our defensive techniques as we demonstrate in the dojo, much less take break fall. Aikido is beautiful at higher levels, when both uke and nage are able to deliver a well-executed attack and defense. Most attackers will fall and stumble most awkwardly, unless properly trained. Even then the risks of real ukemi are much higher.

There is nothing wrong with being a cooperative uke in the dojo. We are there to learn from one another. Egos are to be left at the door. What sets Aikido apart from other martial arts, is that each practitioner experiences both roles – as attacker (uke) as defender (nage). We allow our minds to remain free and open to new ideas and establish harmony within our training. Fighting one another is not what harmony is about.

Do I Need to Break Fall?
One of the first things we do as new students of Aikido is begin instruction in the art of ukemi - falling. We learn various methods of falling: front fall, front roll, back fall and break fall. As beginners we are all in awe of more advanced students taking large ukemi from various techniques. All of us practice very hard to accomplish such achievements. Over time, sometimes completely unaware in our quest to play with the big boys and soar high, every ukemi we take becomes a break fall.

We have spent all this time learning to break fall and it has not been easy. So why not use it? The true challenge then, is when to break fall and when to employ standard ukemi. There will be times when break falls are necessary to protect you from nage's powerful technique. But there are also times when nage's techniques may not be as powerful and will require a standard ukemi practice.

Why take the impact of a break fall if it is not necessary? Many of us plan to do Aikido long into our old age. Aikido can be a very high impact pastime especially if you tend to break fall consistently. Only fall as hard as you are thrown. Do not attempt to put additional strain or stress on the body. Break fall when necessary, but allow yourself the opportunity to blend with your partner, so as to feel their true intent. Get connected to the movement.

We train in ukemi practices as a way to defend and preserve ourselves even in the event that we are overcome or have lost balance. But choosing when it is necessary to take the big fall and when not to will be yet another step in developing a feeling connection of mind and body.

Learning to maneuver our way through life can be a life saving skill. It can save us heartache and grief and enable us to make the most of each moment. We will all experience the ups and downs. But like ukemi in Aikido training, the ability to receive the moment as it happens, sense its true intentions, can help gain new insights and create better relationships. Ukemi teaches us to create an out if the situation is too much to handle. In life, we become aware of the times when we should just step aside and let things unfold. Ukemi also prepares us for the possibility that a fall may be inevitable and instructs us on how to make the best of it. Life will surely throw these times at us as well. Knowing we can recover and continue on creates a lasting hope for the future.

XI. Randori
- Dealing with Multiple Attackers

The Essence of Randori

Randori is a free practice dealing with multiple attackers. It is a drill that promotes the principles of movement, connection and control of energy – energy that is directly in our path. It is a study of motion within Aikido – constant motion.

Randori enhances focus. It increases body awareness, area/environment awareness and people/thing awareness – in Aikido's case the uke and the nage.

When approaching randori we must keep in mind it is a drill – a drill of movement within constant motion. This motion is created by uke and nage and it is the connection of the two that enhances the drill and the movement – it is the dynamics of the two that hone a true understanding of the essence of Aikido.

Randori is an exercise that is designed for both uke and nage – not just nage which many people think. Without one you cannot have the other. Without the union of the two there is no exercise, thus, no learning.

Uke is challenged to commit to the attack and to learn to trust in their ukemi skills – responding in an instant to the sudden change in direction that nage initiates but that uke created. Uke learns to give up their idea of control and rely on the feeling of movement to lead them, again created by nage. Uke does not determine when and where they fall – nage does. It is then uke's responsibility to protect themselves during the fall. Unless uke gives themselves to the movement the drill is not beneficial to anyone. Uke's role is crucial. Uke's relationship to time and space is what forces nage to begin their maneuvering through the labyrinth of moving obstacles. Uke must also learn to deal with other uke – maneuvering around them to get to nage - being aware of falling bodies – being aware of their space and their relationship to the exercise.

Nage learns to respond to multiple situations, and within a confined area that may also be filled with a number of stationary and/or moving obstacles – in this case uke being a moving obstacle. Nage is challenged with moving around in a constant flow and state of movement – both from themselves and from uke. Nage must weave themselves in and out of the obstacles without allowing to be pushed back or caught. Like a game of chess or pool, nage must be three to five moves ahead - being in the moment but living in the game - adapting as needed. Nage must constantly move forward even if they are forced to move back. Think of it as that large rubber band that wraps around your waist – it snaps you back like a slingshot. Nage must learn to dictate the pace of the attacks - controlling distance and timing. Using a variety of Aikido basics, tenkan, kaiten, irimi, nage moves about connecting, directing and redirecting uke as they encounter one another, letting uke pass, taking the path of least resistance.

Nage must control the flow, moving to the outer edge and always towards uke – not allowing uke to push them back or limit their potential to escape.

Even though nage must be several moves ahead, they must deal with one uke at a time. So to do this nage must "divide and conquer" - always moving to the outside, nage moves to the far ends of the circle keeping uke to one side - always moving away from the center of the circle as not to be trapped in the middle. This movement allows for a better view and helps set the pace. Nage must never wait for uke to advance to them but advance to uke – forcing them to react. Nage may use one uke to evade another – always moving forward – in thinking and in physical motion.

Our daily routines throw many things at us. We are confronted with one situation after another. Randori training can enhance our response time and our ability to resolve what life throws our way. It shows us how to stay focused and stay calm in the face of adversity. Randori teaches us how to create an acceptable pace – one that allows us to find the good in a situation. This multiple attacker scenario demonstrates that we must constantly keep moving to avoid getting caught up in the mundane and trivial aspects that we and others create each day for ourselves. Randori as an everyday means makes us more aware of everything and everyone around us, and gives us the tools to successfully interact on a personal and social level.

XII. Changing Direction
- Paths of Least Resistance

The best way to avoid a conflict is to get out of the way. Aikido teaches us to allow an oncoming obstacle to pass rather than meeting it head on. We learn movements like body shift and circle step, to allow a person's energy to pass us. We learn to blend and "go with the flow" instead of resisting. These principles taught on the mat can be carried over to everyday situations. For instance, if you have plans to visit a friend's house after school or work but your parent's car or your own breaks down making you unable to go, then go with the flow. Say *"OK"* and *"maybe we can reschedule"*. By using what Aikido teaches us, we will be able to "go with the flow" and overcome any conflict.

Everyday we experience something new. We confront new challenges, new choices and hopefully make new friends. But along the way we also make mistakes. This is a part of life – a part of growing. Mistakes help us learn how to do something different or better. Mistakes should never be looked at as failures but as stepping stones to a better you.

When we start Aikido training, we find many of the movements strange and awkward. We have difficulty trying to remember everything the instructor said and showed. We may even find that we are doing the technique incorrect. Sensei may come over and remind us to step with our back foot or to remember to move out of the way. Sensei may even show a different way tailored for our own personal understanding – to help in learning.

When doing something new, it is always expected to make mistakes. Many times making mistakes is a good thing. Mistakes lead to growth and growth is a positive thing as long as we are open to it. So the next time you are on the mat allow yourself a mistake and learn from it.

Take the Body Out
Aikido deals with many aspects of confronting an advancing oncoming attack – over head strike, side strike, kicks and punches. Sometimes we get so caught up in the attack itself we seem to focus on the attacking appendage to the point that we forget that it is attached to someone. This someone, uke, possesses a considerable

amount of power and strength especially when in the process of advancing with a committed weapon.

This over-focus can inhibit our perception and ability to deal with the overall attack. We must realize that the attack is not necessarily coming from uke's appendage but rather from the body of the person who is using the particular appendage to do the work. The power generated for the attack is really coming from the center, the hips and the forward momentum of uke. If we concentrate not on the appendage as the source of attack but the presence of mass driving it, we assume by taking the "body" out of the arm or whatever weapon is being used, we would diffuse the weapon's strength and power. In turn, we would control not only the weapon but the body controlling the weapon as well. Once we control the weapon, we create a direct link from our body mass centerline to uke's body mass centerline, channeling our energies to subdue both weapon and wielder.

You will find that this simple yet highly effective technical assertion to your movement and thought process will not only increase your technique insight but will enhance the power of your entry, lead and control.

Plateaus
Everyone experiences them and they are a very important part of our Aikido training. Plateaus give us a point of reference on how our techniques are evolving and where we stand in our training. They define our growth. As this roller coaster ride takes you through, you will find that the ups and downs are fewer but longer between. In the beginning stages of our aiki development we struggle with new concepts and develop those concepts to our physical make-up while trying not to fall over. This is quite normal. So as we grasp one thing, a new concept comes along to master. As the years pass many of these basic concepts and movements become natural to us and we think less about them and more about finer points, whereas the plateau brings particular singular gains and in many regards more rewarding ones. Sometimes it is the little things that count and make the big difference.

What is Training Hard?

What is the true meaning of training hard? We sometimes get so wrapped up in the physical aspects of our training we may start to become a machine - one that puts a hurting on our training partners and at times, ourselves. We have accessed all this power but we have not gained the control to use it properly.

Training hard has to do with personal growth through self-challenge. It is more than just physical – it is mental, spiritual and emotional as well. This pertains to self not other students. Training hard is not roughhousing or beating on your fellow Aikido-ka. It is not winning at all costs and it is not about domination or control of others. Training hard is a commitment to further who you are, discover what you can achieve, and embrace what is around you.

It is a test of courage, inner strength, responsibility, mental awareness and focus. It is a test of the human character. We must push ourselves to our limits – then beyond. Training hard is a constant re-evaluation. Where we are today is not where we were yesterday and not where we will be tomorrow. Training hard is never giving up, not accepting defeat and never expecting to fail. The journey is endless but so are the rewards – if we allow ourselves the chance to reap them. Train hard!

A Better You, a Better Me, a Better World

Throughout life there will be conflict: conflicts with governments, with the environment and with family, friends, neighbors and ourselves. Conflict is an essential part of life. There is nothing we can do to change that. Many times great changes come from conflicts. But how we deal with conflict in our daily lives is the one aspect we can control. We choose how we want to react. Do we get all frustrated and blow up each time conflict enters our space? Or do we step back, take a deep breath and examine the situation?

People will disagree - there's no changing that either. But we can learn to see what the other person sees. We can allow others the opportunity to express their views and ideas without the fear of being attacked because of them. And if we do this for others, they will eventually do the same for us.

This is what Aikido teaches us - to see what the other person sees; to take a step aside, giving ourselves a moment to reflect before we jump right into something. Aikido makes us aware of the people around us and makes them aware of us.

Everyday is a new beginning. Everyday we learn something new about the world around us and about ourselves. It may be the smallest of things but something new nevertheless. We may find that we can run a bit faster or jump a tad higher. We may have learned a new word or phrase or finished reading an exciting story. Maybe we traveled to a new place, tasted a new food or made a new friend. Whatever it is, we found it in the new day.

Everyday should be looked at as new challenges to conquer – new worlds to explore. A chance to do it right and make it better.

With the start of each New Year, many people make promises to themselves that things will be different. They do all they can, not to repeat the steps of the year prior. Unfortunately, many people give up before they have given themselves a chance to succeed. Change does not come easy, especially if it is change for the better. We must work hard to improve the person we are. And this is not something that can be done in a few weeks or months. It takes time – maybe a lifetime. But the point is you are doing rather than just thinking about it.

Make goals that are reachable. Make the reward a better you. Challenge yourself with each new day to build on what you have learned from the previous day. Only you can reach your goals. Only you can become the person you want to be. Don't count yourself out if things get hard, count yourself in, make a new goal to weather the storm and press on. Challenge yourself everyday!

Everyday should be looked at as new

challenges to conquer – new worlds to explore.

A chance to do it right and make it better.

XIII. Together We Learn Together We Grow

Character Building

Character is what makes you, you. Every person is unique, setting them apart from others. Some people are kind, courageous, independent or cooperative. Many things help in building these traits in us - parents and family, school and friends, life experiences and activities. Aikido is one of those activities that lend a hand in positive character development. Aikido teaches us to work with one another in accomplishing our goals. Aikido teaches us acceptance of the differences life has to offer. Aikido teaches us to be cooperative and not to fight. It teaches us to get along and be responsible for others and ourselves. It shows us that true courage is knowing when to be kind and thoughtful to others. Aikido teaches us to be the best person we can be on and off the mat.

When in Doubt

There come times in every practitioner's training when self doubt seems to shadow over us. It can come at anytime. The questioning: "Am I ready?", "Am I good enough?", "Did I really do my best?", "Was I deserving of that promotion?". All said one time or another and all very valuable questions.

Everyone experiences ups and down in training, like a roller coaster but we may feel more of the downs than ups. This is very normal and it is also normal to question one's performance. This is a long journey, as life is, we will break a lot of yolks before we achieve the perfect egg. This questioning cycle is healthy and a good learning tool. By questioning, we begin to analyze what we are doing and make efforts to correct or advance our techniques. Those who do not question suffer from lack of progressive growth. We learn, progress and grow in steps. We reach plateaus and will not journey further until we are ready. The more questions, the more answers; the more learning, the more knowledge.

With Aikido, the Founder's vision of harmony comes to life. He believed that through Aikido - its practice, both in techniques and philosophies - carried over to everyday life, the world would be saved. As practitioners and keepers of the faith, it may be our responsibility, especially at crisis times, to take what we have learned on the mat and bring it to the world around us. Instill this vision of hope and harmony for the future into others - maybe not by demonstrating nikkyo or sankyo but by demonstrating acts of kindness, understanding, patience and tolerance. Always be mindful of others. Working to understand others may change our view of both them and ourselves.

Waiting on the World to Change
Why does the world have to change first before we decide to do anything? Why wait? It has become the way of the day – waiting around and talking about things but not acting upon them - waiting for others to start, to take the chance, while we sit, watch and criticize - when all the while we could have spent that precious time making our own changes – in our own immediate world.

Once we as individuals change – something amazing happens – the world around us changes – the people around us change – everything is affected – it becomes change making change. So if we wait for the world to change, we run the risk of the worst happening – and that is nothing.

For some of us who have made the choice to attend budo training, Aikido is that change. The Founder believed that Aikido was the way to reconcile the differences in the world. On the mat this is true – people from different walks of life gather together and help each other learn the benefits of Aikido. For us, we have made our decision to change through Aikido - and how Aikido affects our lives causes change, and those affects of change cause others around us to change. No need to wait - change is just around the corner wanting to be found.

On My Way to Aikido
When asked where we are going, we reply, "I am on my way to Aikido" or "I'm going to Aikido". We say this as if Aikido was a place, some tangible object we can hold. But in reality Aikido is not a place. It's not even the destination. Aikido is nothing but a path we follow to enlightenment – personal enlightenment - each being different, a personal achievement unique to the journeyman.

Aikido, as an art, the dojo in which you train, the instructor who aids you and your fellow students, are all but vehicles or tools to help us on our quest. They are the means to an end – where we only begin again. This is but one cycle, one leg of the journey. More than physical, we need a strong, committed and confident mindset, a determined spirit and a dedicated soul. The goal is not what we get but what we become – to others and to ourselves. If we view our training as just going to a place and sweating then we miss the big picture. The more we learn the less we understand hence our learning continues.

So why are we here, using Aikido as our training method – our path? The answer: to gain a better understanding of who we are. Aikido is not a place nor is it for those who do not wish to truly embrace what unknowns lay ahead of them. It is not an easy journey but one with many rewards. And one that you will not travel alone.

Balance

With every new day, each one of us should have a goal – a focus that allows our mind, body and spirit to work on working together. This focus, this oneness, helps us attain a deeper understanding of ourselves and all that surrounds us.

A daily focus could simply be balance. Balance of the mind, body and spirit. Balance of our lives on and off the mat. Balance with ourselves and balance with others. It is that balance that fuels all that we do, say, feel and express. It is through balance we reach new levels, receive new clarity and experience new joys of life. Balance opens up the doors of opportunity allowing us to see what lies ahead. It clears the path, our path to personal enlightenment. Without balance we simply are out of balance – teetering on the edge, never gaining a proper footing to take the next step in life. Be balanced.

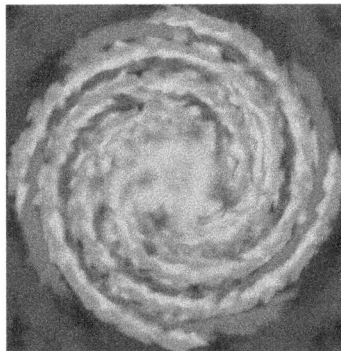

Conclusion: *In the End...*

Mutual Benefit

We hear this term a lot in budo – especially in Aikido – mutual benefit. But what does it really mean to be mutually beneficial? And better yet, is it really happening?

We need first to examine ourselves and our intentions for training and about training. We need to look deep inside to truly answer. Are we there solely for our own personal gain? To some degree, the answer is yes. We are there to learn, to foster new understandings and new relationships and hopefully to cultivate a better self. But is it our only purpose?

If we look back on the pioneers and great masters of old, we will see many who sacrificed much so that others could and would benefit. Selfless actions of courage and endless hours of tired dedication were spent honing their craft - having the diligence to pass what they have discovered on to the next generation.

So looking back we see a life of service – service to their arts and service to others. The end result was two fold. They helped others as they helped themselves, thus, creating mutual benefit.

We grow by aiding others to grow. We learn by assisting others to learn. And we better ourselves by helping others become great.

Mutual benefit is a win, win situation.

Are you a Master in Waiting?

Today it seems like everyone is a master of something. In the martial arts this term is used more and more freely. It seems as though the criteria of what constitutes a master are getting smaller and the master population is growing larger.

Though this may allow people the chance to train with a knowledgeable practitioner of the martial arts, it has become a means by which people limit their training. People hear the term master and they are rushed with a stream of thoughts and beliefs: to be a master one must dedicate their life to a single goal, a single task; one must endure a life of hardships and sacrifice; one must give up all worldly possessions and live in poverty – well maybe not that extreme but you get the idea.

Being a master does involve a part of each of those mentioned above. But the true ingredient is dedication. If the question was asked – "*What is the price of Mastery?*" - there may be many answers given and not all involve money. But dedication would be at the top.

The bottom line is that we need to give of ourselves to achieve – simply put we must be dedicated for it to happen. For some it could take years or it could take only months – regardless we need to be completely dedicated – mind, body and soul.

There is no real measure as to when one achieves mastership. How can there be? Who's to say? But continuous working and striving to the higher levels is what sets those "masters" apart from the rest.

We are all capable of this – we are masters in waiting. The choice is ours from day one. What are we going to do with the information we are given? How will we choose to use it? Do we treat it like another of life's mundane activities or distractions? Or do we make it part of who we are and how we live and choose to be?

Master is but a word – often used in places and with people who do not deserve it. But what master means and what it holds for those honestly reaching for it goes far beyond a piece of paper signed by an organization in a foreign land.

Look inside and see what lies there. You may be surprised to find a master in waiting.

Lines of Separation
We have become so diverse as an art, as a culture, that we have created a solid line of separation. One that is very difficult to cross. If the urge to experiment or sample something presents itself, many of us have become hard pressed to do so. We stand before ridicule or judgment from our peers or teachers. But for that handful of brave souls who have taken it upon themselves with a great leap of faith, to explore and discover, regardless of public opposition, their efforts have paved the way to new understandings and possibilities.

Then why is it when the common practitioner chooses to do the same, they are met with resistance, rejection and resentment? Is this not an art of harmony? Do we not enhance the experience by reaching out and sharing?

Looking back on the path that has been forged by those who came before, we should be in agreement that there are many ways to achieve the same result - many ways in an ever-changing world. Does this mean one is more right than another? That one's teacher was less skilled or knowledgeable than another? Does one group really do it better? Or because it is different, it is then considered wrong? It all stemmed from the same roots. Again, why all the separation?

It can only be a matter of human involvement whereas we have not truly learned what the art strives to embody in all of us – to harmonize. We are the corrosive element. It seems the human factor creates the lines of separation, shutting down the opportunity to grow with one another.

Understanding that different elements resonate with different people, each having its place for the longevity of the art and its teachings, we will be drawn to similar or dissimilar things. Regardless, a strong concern and focus needs to be given to opening the barriers created by style, organization, lineage and other human elemental obstacles and get back to the core purpose of the art – that *Aikido can change the world* if we would allow it to do so by its original design.

Still Mind

10 Tips to Jump Start Your Aikido Training

1. Aikido is a completely unique activity and different from any other martial art you may have studied in the past. With this in mind, the benefits and often the results of Aikido training may not be immediate. It may take some time, for some, possibly a year or more to see improvements in balance, coordination and movement. You are conditioning your mind, body and spirit, laying the groundwork and building a foundation for a lifetime journey. A black belt is not the goal.

2. Aikido involves two arts: taijutsu- empty-handed techniques performed by nage – the thrower. And the art of ukemi – falling, performed by uke – the receiver. Since Aikido is an interactive art, you will play the lead in both roles. These roles go hand in hand with aiki – harmony - development and understanding. To neglect one you can never truly embrace the other.

3. Success in Aikido lies within its kihon dosa – basic movements. The better you do them, the better your balance, coordination and stability will be. Make time to practice basic movements, rather than going through the motions. Focus and work to make the mind and body connection.

4. Falling is part of the art. You will take falls. The three biggest obstacles when it comes to falling are: fear, commitment and ego. Too much fear, too little commitment and too much ego will hinder ukemi development. Allow yourself to let go and trust what you can do. Reread #2.

5. Not everyone will get it. Some people may take longer to reach levels of understanding while some may never come to that point, regardless of how many hours they spend training. Do not focus on others' misunderstandings; rather equate the opportunity as a chance to strengthen your foundation. There is always something to learn.

6. Questions are the cornerstone to learning and growth. Too many questions though, can cause confusion, frustration and may take away from valuable mat training time – not just yours but also your partner's and possibly, the entire class. Limit your questions, so you have time to digest the answers and put the new information to practice before querying again. More is not always better.

7. Learn to cooperate by giving way. Aikido is an art based in the idea of harmonizing with another. Resist resistance. Embrace the opposite and give way. The secret lies in breathing and relaxing.

8. Aikido is an artistic rendering of a martial way. It is a living, breathing art. Thus, it is always changing and growing, as are we. Often, certain techniques or particular exercises are demonstrated and taught solely for the purpose of learning a new skill or furthering the understanding of how the mind and body move as one.

9. Aikido revolves around mutual harmony. A civilized and respectful solution is derived from the use of its teachings and techniques, by and for all who are involved. Not everything we do needs to have a winner and a loser.

10. Have faith. To believe we sometimes have to let go of what we feel to be true. We will find that's when the magic happens.

About the Author

Michael enjoys the fluidity of Aikido and focuses on the technical and martial aspects of the art. He believes Aikido encompasses all the arts and is the vehicle by which a martial artist truly becomes well rounded. Along with his wife, Pamela, the two operate *Asahikan Dojo* in Pennsylvania where they work to release the individual path of each student. Asahikan Dojo also publishes *Aikido Now*, a monthly newsletter available online.

Michael holds the rank of yondan in Aikido. He has additional studies in other styles and various forms of defense. His research has taken him to produce the *Aikido – art in motion* DVD series and the *Essential Defense* DVD series which includes the book *Essential Basics of Self Defense*. He is currently working on his next title. Michael is also an artist and Certified Personal Trainer.

More info can be found at www.asahidojo.com

DVDs

Aikido - an art in motion series *with Michael & Pamela Aloia*

Volume I *Movement:* This DVD focuses on the principle of Movement (dosa) and demonstrates several aikido techniques including irimi, sumiotoshi, kokyunage, koshinage, kokyuho, iriminage, kotegaeshi and ukemi.
33 minutes
DVD: $17.99US each plus S/H $4.00US

Volume II *Connection:* Connection is the cornerstone of Aikido development. This DVD offers a variety of techniques to demonstrate Connection and its relationship to movement and execution. 43 minutes
DVD: $19.99US each plus S/H $4.00US

Volume III *Control:* Control is the pinnacle of technique performance. The DVD displays numerous examples of Aikido techniques demonstrating Control through irimi – entering, kuzushi – taking of balance, kake – execution, paths of motion and with ukemi. 32 minutes
DVD: $19.99US each plus S/H $4.00US

The Perfect Storm: a Woman in Aikido *with Pamela Aloia*
In an art where size, strength or gender are not a factor, women make perfect candidates for Aikido training. Through a female perspective, this DVD displays the art's multi-faceted approach to natural but dynamic movement - emphasizing the daily practice of zazen, meditation, for clarity and enhancement of one's training. 30 minutes
DVD: $19.99US each plus S/H $4.00US

Essential Defense System *with Michael Aloia*
Essential Defense, developed by Aloia Sensei, implements self protection through the principles of Aikido in this 3 volume DVD set. Based on five action words: Move, Connect, Strike, Takedown & Control, Essential Defense will build skill & confidence. Approx. 90 minutes
DVD: $29.99US each plus S/H $4.00US

Other DVDs and books
available at www.*asahidojo*.com

www.ingramcontent.com/pod-product-compliance
Lightning Source LLC
Chambersburg PA
CBHW051842040426

42447CB00006B/661